FAITH
AND
AMBIGUITY

Stewart R. Sutherland

SCM PRESS LTD

334 02003 4

First published 1984
by SCM Press Ltd
26–30 Tottenham Road, London N1

Typeset by Gloucester Typesetting Services
and printed in Great Britain by
Billing & Sons Ltd
Worcester & London

CONTENTS

ACKNOWLEDGMENTS

The central chapters of this short book were the script upon which were based the Ferguson Lectures of 1982. My gratitude is due to the electors of the University of Manchester for the invitation to prepare and deliver them. My thanks are particularly owing to my hosts in the Faculty of Theology who provided an intellectually stimulating, as well as a convivial atmosphere, throughout the week during which the lectures were delivered. Sections of some of the chapters have been published elsewhere as follows: Chapter 1 part one was published in the *Yale Review* 1977, Chapter 1 part two was delivered in the Royal Institute of Philosophy Lecture Series for 1982–83 on 'Philosophy and Literature'. The relevant volume, edited by A. Phillips Griffiths is published by Cambridge University Press (1984). Some pages from the chapter on Hume, were drawn from a contribution to the *Philosophical Quarterly* published in April 1983 (Vol. 33). I am grateful to the respective editors for permission to adapt and use this material.

Stewart R. Sutherland

INTRODUCTION
THE GRASSHOPPERS AND
THE GIANTS

The story is told in the Book of Numbers that when Moses and the Israelites approached the land of Canaan after their long sojourn in the wilderness, Moses sent some spies ahead to bring back reports about the land and its people. When the spies returned they brought samples of the abundant fruit of the land. Caleb was impressed by what they had found and urged Moses and the people to occupy Canaan. The spies however, had faint hearts and protested that

> ... there we saw giants, the sons of Anak which came of the giants: and we were in our own sight as grasshoppers, and so we were in their sight (Num. 13.33).

Now in a spectacularly bad piece of allegorical exegesis I am going to suggest that from one angle this presents a picture of contemporary theology.

There are some notable exceptions to such a picture, but by and large too many theologians look at the central provinces of our intellectual environment and prefer to remain outside: too easily would they retreat to the wilderness as grasshoppers before giants. In so doing they lose the riches of our intellectual and cultural inheritance.

These chapters will be devoted to the discussion of five different philosophers and writers who represent different strands of our cultural inheritance which are all theologically and religiously alive today. What they have in common is a willingness to explore the borderlands between belief and unbelief and to review their own position in the light of what those coming from the opposite direction may have to teach them. What they each reject is the sort of caricature which assumes that belief and unbelief are two homogenous wholes which have nothing to say to one another and no ground for common discussion other than that of agnosticism. Equally, however, do they disdain the implications that the only possibility of dialogue is a marshmallow middle ground where the only rule is that you avoid saying what you really think. One of the intellectuals who will be discussed, Albert Camus, protests firmly at the mistakes of such an outlook:

> The other day at the Sorbonne, speaking to a Marxist lecturer, a Catholic priest said in public that he, too, was anti-clerical. Well, I don't like priests who are anti-clerical any more than philosophies that are ashamed of themselves. Hence I shall not try to pass myself off as a Christian in your presence. I share with you the same revulsion from evil. But I do not share your hope and I continue to struggle against this universe in which children suffer and die.

As we shall see, however, there was no barrier implied to proper exploration of the borderlands between belief and unbelief, and his own dialogue with the posthumous writings of Simone Weil is a model of intellectual and spiritual exploration.

But of course it is not without reason that theologians and believers have stood back from direct involvement with their intellectual contemporaries. We might ask for example, What is to be gained by meddling with secular philosophies or systems of belief? Why should the theologian divert himself from the study of the history of his tradition in trying to understand it for his own day? There are many replies to be given to this latter question but I restrict myself to three. In the first place any worthwhile doctrine of man must address itself as clearly to the fruits of the intellect as a doctrine of creation must to the fruits of the soil. In the second place the theologian has not always seen himself as grasshopper before intellectual and artistic giants: nor if we recall Dante and Eliot, Augustine and Butler, can we believe that literature and philosophy have always appeared to be at odds with theology. Finally it does appear to me that the churches today are suspicious and therefore neglectful of intellectuals.

My reply to the former question, What is to be gained by meddling with secular philosophies and systems of beliefs?, will however be less clear in its contours, for it is undoubtedly the case that a theology which enters into dialogue with alternative views of the world does put itself at risk. The theme of these chapters will be the nature and extent of such risk. It will be for you to decide whether the potential disadvantages of such risks outweigh the possible benefits. The title of this book *Faith and Ambiguity* does give some indication of where the crux of the matter lies. The method to be followed is that of a series of case studies.

The role and place of intellectuals in the discussion of religious belief is always a matter of debate and difficulty. As we shall see the difficulty is partly rooted in the intellectuals themselves. Intellectuals are each complex in their own way and no one pattern can be applied to all. In part however, the difficulty lies in the very pervasive picture of the relation between belief and unbelief which dominates the thinking of many an atheist as well as most orthodox believers. It is assumed that believers and unbelievers are divided by a great and virtually uncrossable chasm. Those who see the differences defined in such a picture allow at best the possibility of a dangerous and daring crossing, the favoured metaphor is that of 'a leap', occasionally even more terrifyingly 'a leap in the dark'.

Whether they find themselves believers or unbelievers, intellectuals in general are hardly renowned for the athletic vigour from which such a metaphor draws its robust appeal. More to the point, our case studies will show that the metaphor of the 'leap', and the picture of the great chasm dividing belief from unbelief, ill represent the situation. My argument will be that the boundaries between belief and unbelief are in certain important respects quite unclear. Believers who live close to the boundaries often share more with neighbourly unbelievers than they do with fellow believers who view the pastures of unbelief as far distant and dangerous lands from which they will for ever remain separated. This is true, I am inclined to think, not only of believing and disbelieving *intellectuals*, but it is easier to show this in their case, and my examples for discussion will represent differing but complementary intellectual traditions.

The writers and thinkers whom I shall discuss are not easily characterized collectively, but they are all certainly intellectuals if by that is intended a capacity and inclination to serious and critical reflection on what they believe to be important. Each in their own way regarded the beliefs and practices of religion as demanding such serious critical reflection, and perhaps surprisingly, I shall argue that each is to be regarded as belonging to the intellectual frontiers where belief and unbelief meet and occasionally merge. If I list the examples which I shall discuss, Hume, Kierkegaard, Camus, Simone Weil and Dostoyevsky, it becomes immediately apparent that I have not fallen prey to the liberal dream of a soft centre where differences are submerged rather than discussed. Although I claim all of these as inhabitants of the borderlands between belief and unbelief, I cannot deny that they were all acutely aware of the differences between belief and unbelief.

However as I shall show for example from the case of Camus, his account of the difference between Christianity and atheism is all the clearer because of his deep engagement with the writings of Simone Weil which came, so to speak, from across the border. Equally, Kierkegaard's account of Christian belief owes much of its insight to his desire to analyse and present belief from the standpoint of anonymity, where the beliefs of the author are irrelevant to the reader's perception of the truth of the work. Hume's account of belief draws as much from his congruence of spirit with the Moderate party in the Church of Scotland, as it does from the personal attacks made upon him by the 'unco guid' and the 'unco orthodox'. Dostoyevsky is perhaps the case which most clearly sustains and defines my thesis, for his genius is the expression of the spiritual pain which comes from simultaneously inhabiting the worlds of belief and unbelief.

I

DOSTOYEVSKY

The dilemma of the intellectual who inhabits the borderlands between belief and unbelief is nowhere made clearer than in Dostoyevsky. He is, I shall argue, pre-eminently a man divided, inhabiting simultaneously the worlds of both belief an unbelief.

A biographer or a portrait painter attempt to show us 'the whole man'. In their painstaking detailed creative efforts they try to present us with a unity. The question which I wish to ask of Dostoyevsky concerns the sort of unity which we might hope to find in his case. He was preoccupied, we might almost say obsessed with God and with Christ. Do we find in him then, a unity of belief in God and Christ, or alternatively the unity which might come from the final rejection of both? The answer will be a complex one, as complex as Dostoyevsky's relationship to the characters of his novels. My discussion will initially focus on one example from the greatest of his novels, *The Brothers Karamazov*,[1] and will then proceed to raise more general questions about the nature of the fulfilment which Dostoyevsky's own life found, and its significance for our theme of the borderlands of belief and unbelief. In the first instance, however, we turn to that puzzling and ambiguous treatment of faith, the legend of the Grand Inquisitor.

I

'The legend of the Grand Inquisitor is the high point of Dostoyevsky's work and the crown of his dialectic.' With this judgment by N. Berdyaev, few would disagree. Dostoyevsky himself regarded the legend in this way, referring to it in a letter as 'the culminating point' of the whole novel. Agreement as to importance, however, does not guarantee agreement as to interpretation. The radically divergent interpretations available are not simply as they often may be, largely attributable either to the ingenuity of the professional academic, or to the stimulating but desperate insights of the PhD candidate. Rather are the different responses to the tale a measure of the artistic genius of its author. At one level the tale certainly acts as a mirror to the ideological and theological dispositions of the reader. Whether, at another level, it may also act as a lamp, with which one may inspect the mind and soul of one's society and oneself, is a more searching enquiry to make of any piece of writing.

Dostoyevsky gives us the legend recounted by Ivan Karamazov to his younger brother Alyosha. Ivan, the intellectual, the atheist has returned from Moscow after several years' absence, with a reputation for cleverness, even brilliance. He and his brother Alyosha, a novitiate monk, after eyeing each other for several months, are talking at length for the first time. They are, in the title of an earlier chapter, 'getting acquainted'. In this context Dostoyevsky gives us one of the most searching discussions to be found anywhere in literature, of life and its significance, of good and evil, and of God and man. The setting for such profound themes, in characteristically Dostoyevskian fashion, is not the long straight avenues of Tolstoy's *War and Peace*, with the trees on either side straining toward heaven; nor is it the rarefied and elevated atmosphere of Thomas Mann's *Magic Mountain*; rather it is the backroom of a Russian small-town pub, noisy and doubtless not without odours of its own.

A part of this discussion deals with evil and suffering, particularly the suffering of the innocent. The possibility of an adequate theodicy is rejected by Ivan, and Alyosha, without quite conceding that the ways of God are not justifiable to men, points out that Ivan has made no mention of the man who, in his innocence, took great suffering upon himself – Christ. Ivan, however, has not forgotten Christ: his reply is a poem in prose (Book V, part 5).

Alyosha shall be his 'first reader – that is, listener'. That poem is the legend of the Grand Inquisitor.

It is set in sixteenth-century Seville 'in the most terrible time of the Inquisition, when fires were lighted every day to the glory of God, and in splendid *auto-de-fé* the wicked heretics are burnt'. Ivan visualizes the return of Christ, and although 'he came softly unobserved', walking among the crowds, he is immediately recognized. The response is like that of the crowds at the height of his Galilean ministry. As then, he heals, but he is silent. The Cardinal, the Grand Inquisitor, appears and observes.

> He knits his thick grey brows and his eyes gleam with a sinister fire. He holds out his finger and bids the guards take him. And such is his power, so completely are the people cowed into submission and trembling obedience to him that the crowd immediately make way for the guards, and in the midst of the deathlike silence they lay hands on Him and lead Him away.

Late that night the Inquisitor comes to his cell and there ensues a long monlogue in which the Inquisitor offers both a justification of himself and an indictment of Christ and his teaching.

The burden of his charge against Christ is stated as follows:

> Thou didst think too highly of men . . . for they are slaves, of course, though rebellious by nature. Look around and judge; fifteen centuries have passed, look upon them. Whom hast thou raised up to Thyself? I swear man is weaker and baser by nature than Thou has believed him . . . By showing him so much respect, Thou didst, as it were, cease to feel for him, for Thou didst ask for too much from him . . . Respecting him less, Thou wouldst have asked less of him. That would have been more like love, for his burden would have been lighter.

The Inquisitor and his allies have taken upon themselves to recognize the weakness of men and to correct and complete the work which Christ began. This, however, is at the price of taking from the mass of men and women their freedom. In the end, men are unable to bear the weight of freedom and in return for their freedom, the Inquisitor offers them happiness. In the temptations in the wilderness, he points out, Christ rejected all that could have given him the power to make men happy. He refused to satisfy human hunger by bread made out of stones; he refused the temptation of the spectacular, the diverting, the miraculous leap from the pinnacle of the temple. Finally, he refused to accept the authority of earthly power, the authority which could be his if he had bowed down to his tempter and accepted the sword of Caesar to use it for good.

Instead of these ways to the hearts of men Christ preferred to leave men free to respond to Him or not as they so chose. Instead of miracle, mystery, and authority, with which the Inquisitor sets about 'correcting' his work, Christ has left to men all that is 'exceptional, enigmatic, and vague'. 'In place of the rigid ancient law, man must hereafter with free heart decide for himself what is good and what is evil, having only Thy image before him as guide.' Such a burden is too great for the many. For the few perhaps, for the strong, it is adquate.

> But they only were some thousands; and what of the rest? And how are the other weak ones to blame, because they could not endure what the strong have endured? How is the weak soul to blame that it is unable to receive such terrible gifts? Canst thou have simply come to the elect and for the elect? . . . fifteen centuries have passed, look upon them.

Who is it that loves men? Christ who gives to the many a freedom which the many find intolerable? (As the Inquisitor points out, those who that day 'kissed Thy feet, tomorrow at the faintest sign from me will rush to heap up the embers of Thy fire.') Or is it the Inquisitor who gives to the many both bread and the security which they want (or perhaps 'need'), who loves man the more? He and the few are willing to bear the burden of the knowledge of good and evil, to knowingly choose the way which Christ rejected, and to deceive the people while feeding them, 'declaring to them falsely that it is in Thy name'. The tale ends thus:

> When the Inquisitor ceased speaking he waited some time for the Prisoner to answer him. His silence weighed down upon

him. He saw that the Prisoner had listened intently all the time, looking gently in his face and evidently not wishing to reply. The old man longed for Him to say something, however bitter and terrible. But He suddenly approached the old man in silence and softly kissed him on his bloodless aged lips. That was all His answer. The old man shuddered. His lips moved. He went to the door, opened it, and said to Him: 'Go, and come no more . . . come not at all, never, never!'

These are some of the central elements of this puzzling disturbing tale.

Many have peered into its depths and found mirrored in it their own beliefs and predispositions. The godly have often seen it as a vindication of Christ, and an attack upon some of the many forms of revolutionary socialism being preached in Russia in the mid-nineteenth century. Atheists have argued that it is the final statement of the bankruptcy of Christianity, that the Grand Inquisitor was right in his insistence that,

> the ages will pass and humanity will proclaim by the lips of their sages that there is no crime, and therefore no sin; there is only hunger. 'Feed men and then ask of them virtue!' That's what they'll write on the banner which they will raise against Thee, and with which they will destroy Thy temple.

The tale can and has been seen in even greater variety and detail as an attack variously upon the Roman Catholic Church (the Inquisitor), upon Protestantism (Christ), upon socialism, upon any form of totalitarian regime, or even more widely as, in Philip Rahv's words, a 'total rejection of Caesar's realm, a rejection of power in all its forms, in its actuality as in its rationalizations'.[2] For some this latter includes warnings not simply about Hitler and Stalin, but, as George Steiner insists, 'the vision of the Grand Inquisitor points also to those refusals of freedom which are concealed beneath the language and outward forms of industrialized democracies'.[3] On the other hand many have seen the tale as an attack upon Christianity, upon Christ: for, it is argued, a kiss is no reply at all. This single gesture of reply, whatever its literary elegance, 'has about it', as Steiner argues, 'something of evasion'.

Romano Guardini approaches from a different direction. Whatever Dostoyevsky's intentions (and almost all the commentators feel obliged to use *that* expression or its equivalent at some point), he suggests, 'in the final analysis, face to face with this Christ, isn't the Grand Inquisitor right? Is not this Christ really a "heretic"?'[4] There is here, he claims, a distortion of Christ and his teachings, for this Christ ignores what Guardini calls 'the middle level' and concerns himself with only 'the exceptional', the kind of freedom that brings a perhaps unbearable 'absolute responsibility' for one's own destiny.

There is one pool into which all commentators gaze, but there are many reflections. Perhaps to look for light from within the pool, to hope that it is a lamp rather than a mirror, is a mistake, and in all probability what follows will simply be another set of reflections. I do feel obliged, however, to point out that the commentator whose views I find most sympathetic is the Russian writer Vasily Rozanov, of whom we are told, 'As a child, Rozanov read a great deal and daydreamed. He completed the gymnasium and attended the University of Moscow, where he ridiculed the professors, slept through the lectures, and cheated in the examinations.'[5] Perhaps it will mitigate my attachment to the views of such an ex-student if I tell you that I find his analysis of the legend more penetrating than some of his counterarguments to the Inquisitor.

One fundamental question concerns what we ought to look for in a tale of this sort. It is a mistake, I want to assert, to see it as a political tract dealing solely with the issues of the day, whether our day or Dostoyevsky's. If you want that from Dostoyevsky, you must look to his *Diary of a Writer*, though even there it is a mistake to view it as the source of a political programme. Although this has often been the basis of criticism of Dostoyevsky, if the legend of the Grand Inquisitor were designed to give specific answers to specific political and social questions, it would be a failure. What it does do, however, is raise a series of questions which concern the metaphysics, the presuppositions lying behind *all* human activity. It is also a warning of the dangers inherent in forgetting the importance of these seemingly abstract questions in our total preoccupation with the practical.

Three of the most important of these questions are: (*a*) What is the nature of Christianity? (*b*) What is the nature of human society? and (*c*) What is it to be a human being?

What is the nature of Christianity? This first question is raised by the story rather than *in* the story. I think that there is a fairly clear picture of Christianity offered, and I think that in the end Guardini is right to imply that it is a humanistic and atheistic picture of Christianity and of Christ. The picture, in the Inquisitor's words, is this: 'In place of the rigid ancient law, man must hereafter with free heart decide for himself what is good and what is evil, having only Thy image before him as guide.' There is no mention here of God, of providence, or of the third person of the Trinity. The gift of freedom leaves no room in this conception for grace, or for the activity of God underlying and supporting the activity of men. This is Ivan's conception of Christianity and, at times, I think, it is Dostoyevsky's. Guardini challenges this view of Christ, and certainly whatever its strengths it is not simply an exposition of the teaching of the New Testament. Three issues, however, ought to be raised here, because they are raised by the story.

First, what of the past nineteen centuries – whatever one's view of Christianity? Has Christianity only been for the few, whether the elect, or the strong? Secondly, what place does freedom have within Christianity, either the Christianity of Ivan's sort, or the Christianity which would seek to reconcile freedom with the distraction of miracles, and with the activities of an omnipotent God? Thirdly, for better or for worse, Ivan's view of Christianity is one which is held by many today. The reasons for this are legion. In the context of the novel it has much to do with the suffering of the innocent. If such a view is held, what does one make of the second and third questions concerning the nature of society and what it is to be a human being?

The second general question confronted in the tale concerns the nature of human society. It is a mistake, I think to regard the Grand Inquisitor as, from the outset, wholly and irredeemably evil. He embodies that part of all of us which leads us toward organizing others 'for their own good'. We *all* of us wish to see that a mentally sick person is not treated as a criminal; we *do* wish to help those 'who cannot help themselves'; we often do *not* expect virtue from deprived and hungry people. Often those most in need do not know best what they need, nor how to organize themselves. The disadvantaged depend upon the advantaged, for they do not have the means to retrieve their desperate situation. One of the main disadvantages of the needy is, of course, lack of education. This makes things doubly tricky because if they lack education, they lack the wit to see what *we* see, i.e., what will improve their situation. Perhaps therefore we ought to impose it on them for their own good.

It is easy to move down the same track as that followed by the Grand Inquisitor. We all follow it *part* of the way, or I hope we do. Dostoyevsky's warning prefigures that of Aldous Huxley's *Brave New World* and of George Orwell's *Nineteen Eighty-Four*. Dostoyevsky's warning is perhaps more subtle, for it reminds us that the 'social engineers' are not to be found simply in the ranks of geneticists or biochemists, nor only among the grey men of the Kremlin. They are found potentially in the hearts and minds of all of us, and indeed in the compassion of the Grand Inquisitor for those 'millions and tens of thousands of millions of creatures who will not have the strength to forego the earthly bread for the sake of the heavenly', as well as in the Inquisitor's insistence that he serves 'the weak, ever sinful and ignoble race of man'. Cynical as he may have become, as Ivan tells us, the Inquisitor's first step in this direction was in the name of humanity:

All his life he loved humanity, and suddenly his eyes were opened, and he saw that it is no great moral blessedness to attain perfection and freedom, if at the same time one gains the conviction that millions of God's creatures have been created as a mockery, that they will never be capable of using their freedom.

Is the alternative then simply to release all human beings on a social tide of complete freedom to fend for themselves? That will

Christ recognises the love of the Inquisitor but this reply as always is silent, meaning 'follow my example'. The Inquisitor cannot bear the suffering this involves (D. has no answer to this) and

DOSTOYEVSKY
9
shuts out Christ. But the answer remains, in fact even of this fuller true suffering Christ.

lead in extremes to Thomas Hobbes's conception of a state of nature where life is 'nasty, brutish and short'. In the middle distance it leads to *laissez-faire* economics where the strong, the quick-witted, and the inheritors, stand on the backs of the weak, the meek, and the poor.

In the legend, there are no 'pat' answers to this dilemma: no quick solutions; no panacea awaits round the corner for some bright boy or other to patent. Are we left then with the good old liberal intellectual dream of the power of rationalism and enlightenment, and the avoidance of extremes? This leads to the third of the general questions posed by the tale.

What is it to be a human being? How potent in human life are freedom and rationality? There is a story going around that the liberal intellectual dream of the power of rationalism and enlightenment to limit the excesses of human life was exploded by the assassination of the Kennedys, or of Martin Luther King. This is simply a more recent version of the story that it was exploded by what the advancing Allied armies found in Auschwitz and Buchenwald. An even earlier version of the story is that it was exploded by Dostoyevsky in the heights and depths of his plots, in the extremes of the human psyche displayed in his novels.

Dostoyevsky is not concerned to define what a human being is, nor to give a blueprint for the details of social organization. His genius is to lay before our eyes what men and women can be like, the heights and the depths, the grotesque forms which human society can take if we allow ourselves to be ensnared by stereotypes of human nature. The importance here lies in the questions that we keep asking of these stereotypes, be they fashioned according to the weaknesses of men, or according to the effervescence of some deluded notion of absolute freedom and strength. Russia of the mid-nineteenth century abounded in visions of a wholly new form of society – visions of the way it could be with human beings: as discussed, for example, by the Petrashevsky Circle, for membership of which Dostoyevsky came as close to execution as any man can, and still live, and for membership of which he was exiled to Siberia for four years; or, as variously hinted at or planned in detail by thinkers or writers as diverse as Pisarev,

Belinsky, Chernyshevsky, Turgenev, eventually even Tolstoy. Against their varying conceptions of society Dostoyevsky set the men and women of his novels. What they threw into sharp relief were the contours of the moulds of quasi-human form through which we all had to pass in order to be initiated into these various dreams of utopia. At the stage of writing *Notes from the Underground* Dostoyevsky believed that our innate rebelliousness and our affirmation of human freedom, or even capriciousness, could and would protect us from such systematization. But by the time he was writing about the Grand Inquisitor sixteen years later in 1879–1880 he was less self-confident, even about freedom; more aware that it was something which could be taken from men, and which might even be given away by men. 'In the end,' the Inquisitor insists, 'they will lay their freedom at our feet, and say to us, "Make us your slaves, but feed us".'

One final question: it may seem as if Dostoyevsky leaves us with a wholly tragic vision of human life. Does he? There are, I believe, tragic elements in it. It is in the end a vision of life without God, and for those who have known what it is like to believe in a God, this can have tragic dimensions to it. Rozanov romanticizes Dostoyevsky's position thus:

> One man, who lived among us, but who, of course, resembled no one of us, sensed in an incomprehensible and mysterious way the actual non-existence of another, and before he died, he reported to us the horrors of his soul and his lonely heart, feebly beating with love for the One who is not, and feebly fleeing from the one who is.

Also, I think the hopes which, earlier in his life, Dostoyevsky had attached to the idea of human freedom have clearly undergone a searching analysis. Freedom *is* for the strong: it *can* be taken from men; it can be *given* away, and, of course, since *Brave New World*, and *Nineteen Eighty-Four*, we are more aware than ever of the variety of subtle and at times seemingly irresistible techniques which can be used to deprive us of this freedom.

Most profoundly he was by this time convinced that, even where men do keep alive the germ of freedom within themselves, this constitutes a burden. George Steiner characterizes the burden in this way:

> Men are racked by doubt and metaphysical anguish because Christ has allowed them the freedom to choose between good and evil. This is the central theme of the Legend.

As freedom to protest and rebel is our defence against those who would engineer for us the details of our destiny, so, for Dostoyevsky, that freedom depends upon the wider freedom to choose between good and evil, and indeed to decide what constitutes good, and what, evil, which wider freedoms were for us, he thought, a source of anguish and suffering. That we have it, however, is cause for hope rather than despair. Nonetheless, just as, in a different context, the poet Schiller (whose work was a powerful stimulus to Dostoyevsky) separated hope and bliss as irreconcilables in human life, so too Ivan, whose tale this is, separates the one from the other. The implication of some forms of theism is that we *can* have both, albeit the bliss is not here and now. In separating the two ultimately, Ivan is expounding one of the most subtle and persuasive of the many forms which atheism may take.

II

Thus the Grand Inquisitor, Ivan's creation, presents a Christ-figure whose message is ambiguous. The ambiguity has deep roots and it defines in cameo-form the profound uncertainty of one of the driving forces of Dostoyevsky's thought and writing. This uncertainty is found throughout Dostoyevsky's novels and it was an uncertainty which he never resolved. As such it raises the question of whether in his life and work Dostoyevsky found fulfilment.

My argument is that the ambiguity of the Christ-figure is the ambiguity of Dostoyevsky's own soul. He is quintessentially the man who inhabits the worlds of belief and unbelief. Did he die then, a man torn within and therefore unfulfilled? The answer to that question must await the discussion of what would count as fulfilment for Dostoyevsky.

Philosophers have devoted much attention to a series of issues grouped under the heading 'the problem of personal identity'. In most of these discussions the focus has been the question of identity over time and the issues confronted have been basically logical or metaphysical. Students enrolled in philosophy classes dealing with such topics often express a sense of disappointment or frustration, for of course, they belong to a culture in which the jargon of 'self' or 'personal' identity belongs to a rather different intellectual context heavy with the overtones of existentialism or with the suggestion of psycho-analysis. Anglo-Saxon philosophers have tended to bypass these ways of construing questions of personal identity – sometimes for good reason, sometimes not.

While not questioning the importance of established philosophical ways of discussing personal identity, I have some sympathy with those students who suggest that this is not the whole story. There are many directions from which emerge calls for an extension of the philosophical discussion of personal identity, beyond analysis of identity over time. For example, the philosophy of law, political philosophy and medical ethics all pose interesting and important questions here.

In a rather different context, it is my hope that the content of this chapter will impinge upon the question of personal identity as it arises when we begin to talk about moral integrity, moral consistency and consistency of beliefs. The biographer or portrait painter attempt to show us 'the whole man'. In their painstaking detailed creative effort they try to present a unity. My concern is the case of one individual, Fyodor Dostoyevsky. Is there a unity to be found there? If so, what sort of unity? Can anything useful be said about it? Where would we find it? One way of asking such a question which will at least allow us to begin to discuss it intelligibly, is to ask what would count as fulfilment for Dostoyevsky.

Dostoyevsky died on 9 February 1881 (28 January, old style). How do we view or assess such a man as Dostoyevsky from the perspective of his death? The temptations of the obituary writer extend far beyond the columns of *The Times*. When a man dies, perhaps for our own sake as much as his, we seek to sum him up, to measure his achievement. In the case of Dostoyevsky such a temptation must be resisted.

> The life and work of Dostoyevsky are inseparable. He 'lived in literature'. It was his life's concern and his tragic fate. In all of his works he resolved the enigma of his personality. . . .[6]

Mochulsky's comment gives one clue to the magnetic hold of Dostoyevsky's work over the century since the publication of the last section of his final and greatest novel *The Brothers Karamazov* in December 1880, and his death scarcely a month later in 1881. In so many ways his life and his writing were locked together – whether we think of how much of his own personal obsession was beaten on the anvil of artistic form into the story of *The Gambler*, or whether we hear the tense and exhausted cries of his letters:

> From June 15 to October 1, I wrote 20 printed sheets of the novel (*The Brothers Karamazov*) and published *The Diary of a Writer* in 3 printed sheets. And, still, I can't write off the top of my head; I must write artistically. I'm bound in this to God, to poetry, to the success of what's been written and literally to all the readers of Russia.[7]

Life and writing nourished and were devoured by one another. To the very banks of the Styx, to the outer edges of life itself he was inextricably both man and writer. The last pages of *The Brothers* were sent to the publisher on 8 November 1880: a complete number of the *Writer's Diary* was delivered to the printer on 25 January 1881. That same night he suffered from a haemorrhage caused by moving some furniture in his study. Despite further haemorrhaging he was able on 27 January to spend some time with a sub-editor responsible for printing the *Diary*. The next day, in the evening, he died.

The final year of his life brought his greatest literary triumphs. Apart from the completion of *The Brothers* his most ambitious work, within his own time and amongst his own people the great 'Pushkin Address' of 8 June was a moment of unique public recognition. He wrote to his wife,

My speech was this morning ... The hall was crowded to the doors. No, Anya, no, you can never imagine the sensation it produced.[8]

And sensation it was, both emotionally for those present, intellectually as a bridge between the warring Slavophiles and Westernizers, and in literary terms in the responses and counter-responses which it provoked. Few literary figures can have experienced such climax, such fulfilment, such 'completion' we are almost inclined to say, in the last months and weeks of their lives. The temptation to look to the Aristotelian and Medieval notion of a *telos* realized, is indeed great. Dostoyevky's achievement is immense; it is seminal; it is formative for the generations to come. The life and the literature symbolically came full-circle together.

But in such a bewitching picture we slip backwards too easily from the nineteenth century to a world whose death knell was sounded pre-eminently in the novels of Dostoyevsky. It would be strange indeed for his death to 'round off' his life *so* neatly and *so* carefully as almost to negate the uncertainty, the ambiguity, the dialectic of his literary presence and creation. The fulfilment, the triumph of the completion of his greatest novel, of the impact of his Pushkin Address, these should not mislead us into looking for a false unity and uncharacteristic singularity of perspective – in the thoughts and words of the man who told the tale of the Grand Inquisitor.

Dostoyevsky towers above and defines the nineteenth century in his definition of the multiplicity of the human mind, the multiplicity charted in what Bakhtin refers to as the polyphonic form of his novels. The issue of what constitutes human identity, what gives a human life wholeness, and unity of form, is a central preoccupation of the novels and is defined simultaneously in both content and form. It would indeed be surprising if his death gave to his life the unity and singularity of a *telos* fulfilled – a unity and singularity which he could not find for the heroes of his novels. Yet it would be foolish and blind to deny his achievement, his 'success' if you will, both in terms of external recognition, and in terms of artistic creation. One way of attempting to resolve this apparent paradox would be to define the undoubted unity and fulfilment in artistic terms: but such a path would lead us eventually away from Dostoyevsky rather than towards him. Artist as he was, wholeness for him could never be defined in terms of what Kierkegaard called the 'aesthetic'. Indeed his ridicule of degeneration was at least as strong when applied to literary pretension, as when applied to revolutionary fanaticism. The mayhem of dreams of a false political foundation for society is mirrored in *The Devils* in the anarchy of Mrs Lembke's 'festive day' – beginning ominously in 'a literary matinee, from Twelve to four o'clock', and ending catastrophically at the centrepiece of the evening ball – 'a literary quadrille'.

It would be difficult to imagine a more wretched, vulgar tasteless and insipid allegory than that 'literary quadrille'. Nothing less suitable for our public could have been devised; the quadrille was made up of six miserable pairs of masks – not really masks even, for they all wore the same clothes as everyone else. Thus, for instance, one short, elderly gentleman in a frock-coat – in fact, dressed like everyone else – and a venerable grey beard (tied on – this constituted the whole of his fancy dress) was bobbing up and down on the same spot as he danced with a stolid expression on his face, working away as fast as he could with his feet without moving an inch. He emitted curious sorts of sounds in a soft but husky bass, and it was that huskiness of his voice that was meant to suggest one of the well-known newspapers. Opposite this mask danced two giants X and Z, and these letters were pinned on their frock-coats, but what the X and Z meant remained a mystery. The 'honest Russian thought' was represented by a middle-aged gentleman wearing spectacles, a frock-coat, gloves and – manacles (real manacles). Under the arm of this 'thought' was a brief-case containing documents referring to some 'case'. An opened letter from abroad to convince the sceptics of the honesty of the 'honest Russian thought' peeped out of his pocket. All this the stewards explained by word of mouth, since it was impossible to read the letter which protruded from his pocket. In his raised right hand 'the honest Russian thought' held a wine-glass, as though he were about to propose a toast. Close at each side of him two short-haired nihilist girls capered and vis-à-vis danced another elderly gentleman in a frock-coat, but with a heavy cudgel in his hand, apparently representing a very redoubtable periodical, though not a Petersburg one: 'I'll wipe you off the face of the earth!' But though armed with a cudgel, he just could not bear the spectacles of 'the honest Russian thought' fixed intently upon him and tried to look away, and when he did his pas de deux, he twisted and turned and did not know what to do with himself, so much, apparently, did his conscience prick him . . .'[9]

The door opened regularly since then, of seeking unity, identity and integrity of life in pursuit of the aesthetic was a door through which Dostoyevsky refused to pass.

Even in his death, it seems, Dostoyevsky has left us with a legacy of ambiguity and uncertainty. Yet even if, to change the metaphor, we cannot see his death as the final line drawn in an account of his life, which, drawn after a year of spectacular achievement and recognition, leaves the bonus or credit which gives unity, identity and meaning to his life, there remains an alternative perspective in which the relation of life to death, for Dostoyevsky, is itself a parable. His death did not come out of season, nor yet, however, did it come at the completion of the circle of seasons from the spring of birth to the autumn of death. Such a picture of life and death (the latter being 'in season' or 'out of season'), has virtually been lost in our culture, and Dostoyevsky foresaw this in many ways. The rest of this lecture will be devoted to discussing one of the most central ways in which he delineated this – in life and in literature – namely in his treatment and expression of religious belief.

Those who would see his death as giving completeness to his life, and who thus picture the life as a unity, the race having been run, the battle finished, are paralleled by, and indeed often are, those seeking in his religious beliefs a single, 'complex' perhaps, but 'unified' certainly, religious outlook. From his writings, his novels, his letters, the journalism of *The Diary of a Writer*[10] they cull quotations and references and build up *the* picture of Dostoyevsky's beliefs. He is enlisted in, or vilified for belonging to, a variety of religious causes, the one common feature of each of which is the clarity and certainty with which they can be stated. Very often such pictures of his beliefs can be supported by considerable textual evidence, but I believe such pictures to be wholly misconceived. It is not simply that they are overdrawn on this point, or too emphatic on that: rather they misconstrue entirely the issue which they raise. Let us consider two such pictures each of which in its own way has been immensely influential.

In the same year as Karl Barth published the second definitive edition of his *Epistle to the Romans*[11] his close friend Edward Thurneysen published a short account of Dostoyevsky's religious views.[12] There is more here however, than historical coincidence, for Barth said of Thurneysen that he

> . . . was the one who first put me on the trail of . . . Dostoyevsky, without whose discovery I would not have been able to write either the first or second draft of the commentary on Romans.

Thus in discussing Thurneysen's *Dostoyevsky* we are discussing a picture of Dostoyevsky which played a central part in the most significant redefinition of theology to have taken place in this century.

As befits a man whose stimulation Barth acknowledges in the Preface to the second edition of *The Epistle to the Romans*, Thurneysen builds his account of Dostoyevsky round two fundamental general themes. On the one hand he stresses the undoubtedly dialectical character of Dostoyevsky's work, but, as I shall argue he sees only part of the dialectic. On the other hand he insists that what gives his work 'that absolutely conclusive character, that character so superior to Ibsen, Strindberg, Jacobsen' is its foundation upon 'Biblical insight'. Again I do believe that Dostoyevsky had deep insight into the writings of the New Testament, but I also believe that his insights differed in character from those of Thurneysen or the early Barth.

To be fair however, Thurneysen and Barth did capture much of what is truly Dostoyevskian. They were right to stress his critique of religion and the church. They were correct in their diagnosis of many of his characters as 'yearning for something that is not accessible to man's grasping'; and in their realization that whatever the excesses of his characters, Dostoyevsky's own touchstone of their adequacy is realism; and that for him the extremities of the human spirit point towards rather than away from reality. Thurneysen however, was wrong, in two crucial respects: he was selective in what he culled from Dostoyevsky, and he misinterpreted the significance of the ending of both *Crime and Punishment* and *The Brothers Karamazov*. The second of these points is contentious and I shall return to it later.

The picture which Thurneysen offers is that of a Protestant, neo-orthodox Christian. It may well be that Dostoyevsky's characterization of nineteenth-century Protestantism is quite congenial to both Barth and Thurneysen:

> Protestantism with gigantic strides is being converted into atheism and into vacillating, fluent, variable, (and not eternal) ethics.[13]

Indeed Barth could happily have used such a text as a motto for his *Protestant Theology in the Nineteenth Century*. However what those who see the Protestant principle at work in Dostoyevsky do completely ignore, is Dostoyevsky the Slavophile, for whom the notion of a Russian Christian, and at times perhaps a Russian Christ, has more than illustrative or metaphorical force.

This raises the central question of whether there is a unitary single core of beliefs which can be referred to as Dostoyevsky's religious beliefs. My initial suggestion is that if there is, it will not turn out to be the neo-orthodox Dostoyevsky of Thurneysen's reading of the novels. What then of Dostoyevsky the Russian journalist, editor and author of *The Diary of a Writer* or Dostoyevsky the letter–writer? This is the Dostoyevsky who contrasts most fiercely at times, in accents both nationalistic and partisan, Western Europe where 'the peoples have lost Christ'[14] and

... our people (who) know their Christ God – perhaps even better than we, although they did not attend school. They know, because throughout many a century they have endured much suffering, and in their sorrow, from the earliest days to our time, they have been accustomed to hear about this Christ God of theirs, from their saints who laboured for the people and who defended the Russian soil – sacrificing their lives.[15]

Nor must we be misled by the construction of the sentences. In talking of 'their' Christ God, Dostoyevsky is putting between himself and them, the distance of admiration rather than the distance of Westernizing disdain.

Increasingly in the letters of the 1870s and in the *Diary* Dostoyevsky gave voice to a mystical belief in the recuperative and transforming powers of the Christ of the Russian peasant. Of course he had no illusions about the peasants, and he saw all too clearly the way in which some within the Orthodox Church encouraged their superstition – recall Father Ferapont, in *The Brothers Karamazov*, who so envied the saintliness of Zossima. And yet in his letters and journalism, time and again he sets the Russian Christ and the Russian believer over against all the evil and destructive elements brought into Russia from Europe by the intelligent and the fashionable. He selects his targets and pins his colours to the mast in the opening editorial of *The Citizen* in 1873.

In days gone by ... the words 'I understand nothing' meant merely ignorance on the part of him who uttered them; yet, at present they bring great honour. One has only to declare with an open air and uppishly: 'I do not understand religion; I understand nothing in Russia; I understand nothing in art' – and at once one is lifted to lofty heights.

He also defines the rules of the game as including irony by adding

And this is all the more advantageous if one, in fact, understands nothing.

His targets are those intellectuals who are bemused by Europe into believing that no good can come out of Russia (the Russian boys and their professors whom Ivan Karamazov pillories). The strength of his case against them, he believes, is the faith of the Russian peasant appropriated through centuries of labour, toil and suffering. At times it is as if this alone constitutes the providence of God. Of this intensely nationalistic and sectarian response to the spiritual ills of his time, Thurneysen makes no mention.

Which then, if either, is the *real* Dostoyevsky? At times Dostoyevsky himself seems in no doubt and in 1876 he wrote from Bad Ems in Germany to Vsevolod Solovyev (brother of Vladimir the philosopher),

> The June number of the *Diary* pleased you, then. I am glad of that, and for a special reason. I had never yet permitted myself to follow my profoundest convictions to their ultimate consequences in my public writing – had never said my *very last word* . . . So I decided that I *would* for once say the last word on one of my convictions – that of Russia's part and destiny among the nations – and I proclaimed that my various anticipations would not only be fulfilled in the immediate future, but were already partly realized.[16]

What then is Dostoyevsky's 'final word'? According to Thurneysen the final word of Dostoyevsky the writer is a question – 'the questionability of everything human' – but,

> beyond this final word an absolutely final word may be spoken boldly: God would certainly not be God if he were not really the solution.[17]

or again,

> The absolutely final word is resurrection.

On the contrary however, to Dostoyevsky the journalist and letter writer, the final word says little about 'the questionability of everything human'. He is writing of the dispute over Constantinople between the two great imperial powers of the day – Russia and Britain.

This would be a genuine exaltation of Christ's truth, preserved in the East, a new exaltation of Christ's Cross and the final word of Orthodoxy, which is headed by Russia.[18]

The exaltation is the unification of all the Slavs under Russia and a Russian garrison in Constantinople! Ought we to conclude then that Dostoyevsky the Russian nationalist is the 'real' Dostoyevsky, as his letter quoted above, and his journalism throughout, seem to imply.

It seems time to reflect on the course of the argument so far. The question of the 'real' Dostoyevsky is raised by his death and how we see that. Is his death the sign, as in many outward ways it is, of his *telos* fulfilled – his great work written, his Pushkin address re-defining the central cultural argument of his nation and time – between Slavophiles and Westernizers? If so, we may set about the question of summarizing and tabulating his views, including giving clear statement to his religious beliefs. The essential difficulties of that view however, are twofold: on the one hand it is to negate all that his novels teach us – of the dualities of the spirit, of the ambiguities of character, and of the uncertainties of the human mind; on the other it is to raise the question of which of the many Dostoyevskys to be found in the interpreters is the real Dostoyevsky – for example Dostoyevsky the neo-orthodox theologian (Thurneysen and Barth) or Dostoyevsky the Russian Christian?

My contention is that Dostoyevsky's death, as much as his life and writing, forces us to re-assess what we mean by such terms as 'telos', 'fulfilment' or 'completion'. As a corollary of this, the issue of what a man 'really' believes is also open to re-definition, in terms of both the nature and the content of belief. The beliefs of a club, or a political or ecclesiastical party may be easily, even if temporarily, summarized in a creed. One of the lessons which Dostoyevsky taught is that this is not equally true of individual human beings. His death, as I shall argue, points to the same truth.

In all outward, or (to use Kierkegaard's term) 'world-historical' ways, one might regard Dostoyevsky's life as embodying figuratively even if not numerically, the sense of completion of the biblical 'threescore and ten'. Inwardly however, the appropriate religious metaphor is *pilgrimage* rather than completion. At the time of his death Dostoyevsky's mind and spirit were not at rest. He had not reached a steady or motionless state. He was still in the process of giving form to possibilities of life and belief. It is perhaps not too strained to suggest that not one, but many Dostoyevskys died in February 1881.

The Dostoyevsky we find in Ivan Karamazov, as well as the Dostoyevsky of his brother Alyosha, lived and died together within the one human body. This is true also of the Dostoyevsky we find within the Russian sainthood of Father Zossima, as well as in the energy and spirit of the equally Russian Mitya Karamazov. Neither Dostoyevsky the man, nor Dostoyevsky the artist will be confined to the views of one of his characters. What then of Dostoyevsky the journalist? Do we not find portrayed there the *real* Dostoyevsky?

Now perhaps we can see that in the end our question is hermeneutical in character. The issue which confronts us is one which we face in the interpretation of any set of texts: how do we balance one set of writings against another? – (the *Diary* against the novels?) This, I contend is not a purely technical question for which we can provide a factual or value-free answer. Schopenhauer's comment has much to tell us:

> To estimate a *genius* you should not take the mistakes in his productions, or his weaker words, but only those works in which he excels. For even in the realm of the intellect, weakness and absurdity cleave so firmly to human nature that even the most brilliant mind is not always free of them ... What distinguishes genius, on the one hand and provides a measure for estimating it, is the height to which it was able to rise when time and mood were propitious and which forever remains unachievable to ordinary heights.[19]

My argument is that in Dostoyevsky's case it is in 'those works in which he excels' that we find his deepest insights into human nature – those works, that is to say, dominated by the discipline of what he calls 'artistic realism'. This runs much contrary to the biographical fashions of the day; but the post-Freudian assumption that the heart of a man is best seen in the slips and inconsequentialities of his letters or in the indulgences of his unedited journalism is more often assumed than examined.

Time and time again Dostoyevsky reaffirms *not simply his belief in, but his very bondage to* his art. Recall the letter quoted at the beginning of the lecture where he talked consecutively of being bound to God *and* to poetry. A very famous example of this bears on all of the central issues at stake. The sixth book of the *Brothers Karamazov* is meant to contain the answer of belief to the atheism of Ivan Karamazov. Ivan's atheism is arguably the most powerfully stated in all literature. Understandably Dostoyevsky was deeply concerned about his ability to provide 'a sufficient answer'. His answer was to be the figure of Father Zossima who both fulfils and re-defines the expectations of Russian sainthood. Dostoyevsky's worry was whether he could make such a figure convincing:

> This is what disturbs me, i.e. will it be understood, and shall I achieve even a part of my aim? And there was the further obligation of art: I had to present a modest but august figure, while life itself is full of the comic, and august only in its interior significance, so that in the biography of my monk I was forced, willy-nilly, by the demands of art, to touch on the commonplace and trivial, so as not to mar artistic realism.[20]

Note that the parameters of what it is possible to say by way of response of belief to unbelief are set by the 'obligations of art', but that the art in question is dedicated to 'artistic realism'.

The 'real' Dostoyevsky was bound to the constraints of his art, which in turn were defined by the search for absolute realism. Absolute realism, however, is not to be understood purely in terms of 'social' reality nor in the more parochial concerns of 'kitchen-sink' drama: absolute realism is the portrayal of the inner life and it is at this point that the truth of Mochulsky's assertion that, 'the life and work of Dostoyevsky are inseparable', is most apparent. The concerns of Dostoyevsky the artist and Dostoyevsky the pilgrim are here bound inseparably together. The problem which he faced in giving the Russian saint, Father Zossima, authentic form, *is* the problem of the possibility of belief which is 'sufficient answer' to Ivan. It is also the same problem as those which respectively dominated his portrayal of Sonia in *Crime and Punishment* and Prince Myshkin in *The Idiot*.

In the end he saw the life of faith only as a possibility not as a reality defined. In his novels successively in the characters of Sonia, Myshkin, Father Zossima and Alyosha Karamazov, he attempted to define the nature of human goodness, the goodness of the incarnate Christ. But, and here is where I must seriously part company from Thurneysen (and indeed many of Dostoyevsky's 'Christian' interpreters), Dostoyevsky failed, and knew himself to have failed. Both the man and the artist confess this in the very form which he gave to his novels.

The difference between myself and Thurneysen on this point is evident in the following comment:

> And yet the works of Dostoyevsky shine as if illumined from within with the secret, no longer earthly light of a powerful, an ultimate synthesis. Not decline, not contemptuous laughter over men of whom the devil has made fools, but the incomprehensible word of victory, 'resurrection', is the last word of his novels.[21]

In the paragraphs adjacent to this Thurneysen refers to *The Idiot*, *Crime and Punishment*, and *The Brothers Karamazov* to support his view of Dostoyevsky's 'final word' of 'ultimate synthesis' and 'resurrection'. However, he misinterprets these novels quite systematically. There is no 'ultimate synthesis', and the best that is offered is the possibility of resurrection, but that possibility remains a hope rather than an established certainty.

Consider the outcome of these novels and what they have in common. What they share is *not* a conception of an 'ultimate synthesis', but Dostoyevsky's inability to portray one. *Crime and Punishment* is a tale summarized by the title of the novel: there is no mention of a novel called *Crime and Rehabilitation*, or *Sin and Resurrection*. The hope of 'the dawn of a new future, or of a full resurrection to a new life', for Raskolnikov the murderer, and

Sonia the saint and prostitute, is held out, but note the final sentence of the novel:

> But that is the beginning of a new story, the story of the gradual rebirth of a man, the story of his gradual regeneration, of his gradual passing from one world to another, of his acquaintance with a new and hitherto unknown reality. That might be the subject of a new story – our present story is ended.[22]

And of course, it *has* ended without giving form to the nature of this resurrected life. The portrayal of goodness, of sainthood, must await a new story.

This was the task which Dostoyevsky undertook in his novel *The Idiot*, a novel in which his hope was 'the representation of a truly perfect and noble man'.[23] He evidently sees this as the attempt to define clearly the possibility of a Christlike life, but equally evidently he failed. Myshkin, the Idiot of the title, cannot live in open human society. At the end like Sonia, he takes his goodness off-stage, he returns to the Swiss Sanatorium from which he emerged at the beginning of the novel. The possibility of a resurrected life has still not been defined and as such, the powers of evil and darkness still reign.

Dostoyevsky's final definition of the problem and his last attempt to solve it, come in Books V and VI of *The Brothers Karamazov*. In Book V Ivan states an almost unanswerable case for Atheism – based on the suffering of innocent children. In Book VI as we have noted, Dostoyevsky was intent on answering Ivan's atheism by 'an artistic picture', the figure of Zossima. Now whatever his success in the figure of Zossima (and that is much disputed) Dostoyevsky, again by the form of the novel, acknowledges failure. Ivan has not finally been answered. There is no 'ultimate synthesis'. For Dostoyevsky, the true synthesis, the final reply of belief to unbelief can only come in a statement that conforms to the demands of art and reality.

Zossima is not an adequate answer to Ivan, because Zossima still lives within the confines and protection of the monastery. Zossima himself admits this when he tells his disciple, Ivan's brother Alyosha, to leave the monastery, to marry and to live in the community at large, subject to its pressures and temptations. Only if belief survives and defines itself in *that* context has an adequate answer to Ivan's atheism been given. The novel about Alyosha, as indeed a further novel about Mitya, was never written. The task of defining the nature and practice of Christian belief was never completed successfully. There were preliminary sketches, 'cartoons' if you like, in Sonia, Myshkin, and Zossima, but no 'final word'.

That constitutes my case for arguing contrary to the views of Thurneysen (and all those whom he represents), or against those who dismiss Dostoyevsky as ultimately the reactionary Russian nationalist of parts of the *Diary*. My conclusions can be listed under three points.

1. Dostoyevsky offered no final answer to atheism – as he knew, the story which would do that – of Alyosha – remained unwritten and perhaps unwriteable.

2. It is vain then to seek for a 'final word' from Dostoyevsky on the subject of religious belief – the dialectic defined in Ivan and Zossima remained Dostoyevsky's only 'final word' to the grave.

3. Despite the outward signs of success, of fulfilment Dostoyevsky's own death could not possibly be seen as a moment of completion, or in traditional terms, as a sign that his *telos* had been achieved.

We find such conclusions foreshadowed in one of his earlier explorations of the notions of 'self' and 'freedom', *Letters from the Underworld*. There the view is canvassed of man as,

> . . . a frivolous specious creature, and, like a chess-player, cares more for the process of attaining his goal than for the goal itself. Besides, who knows (for it never does to be too sure) that the aim which man strives for upon earth may not be contained in this ceaseless continuation of the process of attainment (that is to say, in the process which is comprised in the living of life) rather than in the aim itself . . .;

> . . . he has an instinctive dread of *completely* attaining his end, and so of finishing the building operation. May it not be the truth that only from a distance, and not from close at hand,

It is certainly correct to say that D. is a pilgrim: but the unrealized goal in Zosima etc. is consistent with Christian life which is always lived with arms outstretched, in a certain desperation. Was this not central to Christ's life?

DOSTOYEVSKY 27

does he love the edifice which he is erecting? That is to say, may it not be that he loves to create it, but not to *live* in it?[24]

Dostoyevsky's life and art are testimony to the impossibility of so 'summing-up' a man, and his death did not alter the message of his life one whit. Perhaps in an indirect and re-defined way, that is the only *telos* or fulfilment which since the time of Dostoyevsky, it has been legitimate to expect. As a novelist Dostoyevsky embodied such a conception. He died if not 'with his boots on'; certainly with his pen in his hand. His 'achievements' were but stages on the way, for his exploration of human goodness, and of the nature of selfhood was incomplete. The ambiguities remained, the uncertainties were redefined, but unresolved. There is in this a form of integrity or consistency, for his writings constitute a profound rejection of precisely those theories of human nature which underpin bad biographies and insensitive obituaries: the self is not like 'all Gaul', a public object divisible into 'three parts'. In so doing they define the most radical form of living between belief and unbelief.

2

DAVID HUME

If Dostoyevsky was a spirit tortured on a rack stretched between belief and unbelief, so Hume – at least the mature Hume – shows every sign of being quite firmly on the side of unbelief. He was to his friends in Paris 'le bon David' – contented, innocent and jolly. To his friends in Scotland he was witty, even facetious on the matter of religious belief but whether as friend or enemy, as fellow countryman or honoured visitor, ever since the publication of his *Treatise* in 1739–40 Hume's reputation had been that of a sceptic and an atheist. In his own day a group of clergymen attempted to have him formally excommunicated from the Church of Scotland and to that end presented the following Overture to the general Assembly of 1756:

> The General Assembly, judging it their duty to do all in their power to check the growth and progress of infidelity: and considering, that as infidel writings have begun of late years to be published in this nation, against which they have hitherto only testified in general, so there is one person, styling himself *David Hume, Esq.*, who hath arrived at such a degree of boldness as publicly to avow himself the author of books containing the most rude and open attacks upon the glorious Gospel of Christ, and principles evidently subversive even of natural religion and the foundation of morality, if not establishing direct Atheism; therefore the Assembly appoint the following persons, . . . as a committee to inquire into the writings of this author, to call him

before them, and prepare the matter for the next General Assembly.

This was the respectable tip of the anti-Hume iceberg which had many even more unpleasant layers.

There was, for example, a pamphlet published under the ominous title 'The Dust Stretched Upon a Death-Bed; or a Lively Portraiture of a Dying Infidel'. It must be confessed that this pamphlet turned out to have been written, not by a Churchman, but by a former student of theology who had himself been excommunicated! What is clear however, is that then as today Hume was regarded as representing the hard-core of unbelief. This prevented him from ever becoming a Professor of Philosophy while lesser men whose works are now justly forgotten were appointed over his head.

Against this popular picture of Hume I wish to set an alternative view which places Hume firmly in the dialogue of the borderlands between belief and unbelief. It is only from such a perspective I shall argue, that we can properly evaluate the uncertain and ambiguous conclusion of Hume's *Dialogues Concerning Natural Religion*. The mood and style of the *Dialogues* or the relevant *Essays* or sections of the *Enquiries* do not belong to the belligerence of the Assembly Overture, let alone the scurrilous pamphlets. Nor does the biographical evidence point to the realities of Hume's engagement with religious questions as best defined by the popular view.

Just as Hume was not at all at home with the fanaticism of some parties within the Scottish Church, so Mossner hints, correctly I believe, that despite the triumphs of his visit to Paris in 1766, neither was Hume quite at one with the militant atheism of the French *Philosophes*. In one of his letters Diderot tells the well-known story of Hume's first visit to meet the formidable gatherings of this remarkable group of men.

The first time that M. Hume found himself at the table of the Baron, he was seated beside him. I don't know for what purpose the English philosopher took it into his head to remark to the Baron that he did not believe in atheists, that he had never seen any. The Baron said to him: 'Count how many we are here'. We are eighteen. The Baron added: 'it isn't too bad a showing to be able to point out to you fifteen at once: the three others haven't made up their minds.'[1]

I do not think that Hume was being wholly facetious here. His scepticism was no more left in his carriage when he visited the radical atheists' lair in the Rue Royale, than when he contemplated the zeal of the evangelical wing of the Scottish Church.

It is equally important to note his respect for what I may call 'ecclesiastical' philosophers such as Bishop Butler and Thomas Reid, and of course many of his closest friends were to be found amongst the so-called 'moderates' of the Church of Scotland – that distinguished band of clergymen of whom Alexander 'Jupiter' Carlyle wrote,

> Who have written the best histories, ancient and modern? It has been a clergyman of this Church. Who has written the clearest delineation of the human understanding and all its powers? A clergyman of this church. Who has written the best system of rhetoric and exemplified it by his own orations? A clergyman of this church. Who wrote a tragedy that has been deemed perfect? A clergyman of this church. Who was the most profound mathematician of the age he lived in? A clergyman of this church . . .[2]

These were men with whom Hume, for all his philosophical scepticism, felt intellectually at home. From his letters it is clear that he much respected one Gilbert Elliot of Minto, an elder of the Kirk to whom he sent for comment early drafts of his *Dialogues Concerning Natural Religion*. What I might call Hume's 'borderlands sympathies' are shown with great clarity in one of his letters written in 1751:

> I have often thought, that the best way of composing Dialogue, wou'd be for two Persons that are of different Opinions about any Question of Importance, to write alternately the different Parts of the Discourse, and reply to each other By this Means, that vulgar Error woud be avoided, of putting nothing but

Nonsense into the Mouth of the Adversary: And at the same time, a Variety of Character and Genius being upheld, woud make the whole look more natural and unaffected. Had it been my good Fortune to live near you, I shou'd have taken on me the Character of Philo, in the Dialogue, which you'll own I coud have supported naturally enough: And you would not have been averse to that of Cleanthes. I believe too, we coud both of us have kept our Temper very well: only, you have not reach'd an absolute philosophical Indifference on these Points.[3]

Such biographical facts do not establish my case, but they are relevant to the interpretation of the *Dialogues* on which my case rests.

The Ambiguity of the Dialogues

Hume's *Dialogues*[4] is a work notorious for the multiplicity of interpretations which it has provoked. The two major questions which interpreters must confront concern on the one hand the conclusion of the work, and on the other the identification of Hume with one or other of the characters. The *Dialogues* are reported by a young man Pamphilus who described the three central participants as follows:

The remarkable contrast in their characters still further raised your expectations; while you opposed the accurate philosophical turn of Cleanthes to the careless scepticism of Philo, or compared either of their dispositions with the rigid, inflexible orthodoxy of Demea.

His conclusion was that

Philo's principles are more probable than Demea's; but that those of Cleanthes approach still nearer the truth.

The first question which confronts the interpreter is whether this is Hume's own conclusion and whether, notwithstanding the comment in his letter to Gilbert Elliot noted earlier, Hume is to be identified with Cleanthes rather than Philo.

Put more generally the question becomes one of whether Hume, castigated in his lifetime as an atheist had not in the end some sneaking regard for, or acceptance of a form of religious belief.

Cleanthes is the exponent of natural theology who defends a version of the argument from design which in turn Philo attacks mercilessly. The ambiguity and uncertainty occur because having apparently overwhelmed Cleanthes in the earlier sections of the Dialogue Philo, the sceptic, seems to turn round completely in the final section. There in a series of comments he seems to concede the heart of Cleanthes' position.

> A purpose, an intention, a design strikes everywhere the most careless, the most stupid thinker . . .

> If the whole of Natural Theology . . . resolves itself into one simple, though somewhat ambiguous, at least undefined proposition, *That the cause or causes of order in the universe probably bear some remote analogy to human intelligence:* . . . what can the most inquisitive, contemplative and religious man do more than give a plain, philosophical assent to the proposition as often as it occurs; and believe that the arguments, on which it is established, exceed the objections, which be against it?

Now this apparent reversal is quite astonishing. Here Philo the sceptic seems to lay aside the detailed brilliance of his counter arguments to Cleanthes and accept the essence of Cleanthes' natural theology. Does it follow therefore that we must see Hume as theist, or at least deist, rather than sceptic and atheist?

The answer to this question is 'No', and in understanding that, we shall discover some essential truths central to our twin themes of the place of the intellectual in the discussion of religion, and of the borderlands between belief and unbelief. In the end I have no doubt that both Philo and Hume belong firmly within the camp of the unbelievers: but what they teach us through what they share respectively with Cleanthes and with the 'moderates', or with Bishop Butler, is how to define more clearly the real differences between belief and unbelief. The catchwords of the pamphleteers, of the religious or atheistical extremes are too crude. These labels, 'theist', 'atheist', 'deist', 'sceptic' are useless until they are defined more closely, indeed until they are given specific content.

The choice of the dialogue-form for the discussion of religious belief was no mere affectation on Hume's part. It was his own recognition of his 'borderlands' situation, and in the end was a reflection of the nature of the conclusions which he would reach. Philo was an unbeliever, but not in the bald direct fashion of the fifteen *philosophes* whose company Hume shared in Paris: Philo was also an agnostic, but again not in the indecisive sense of the three *philosophes* of the same company who had not yet 'made up their minds'. To the contrary, Philo was quite clear about what he did not know and which beliefs he did not accept. For him as for Hume, the gallup-poll question 'Do you believe in God?' was too crude for serious discussion. The important question is '*What is it to believe in God?*', and to that question his response is complex but sharp-edged and clear. Belonging to the borderlands has given to Hume a clearer sight of the differences as well as the similarities between belief and unbelief.

My defence of this view will involve giving some close attention to Part XII of Hume's *Dialogues*. Two of the most significant points about Part XII of the *Dialogues* concern the disputant who is absent – Demea. We are told quite explicitly that Part XII reports the conversation 'after Demea's departure', a point to which I shall return. What seems to me of greater significance however is that in part XII Philo uses on Cleanthes a technique of disputation very similar to that which he deployed against Demea.

Throughout the early sections of the *Dialogues*, as Cleanthes was well aware, what Philo offers to Demea may well be the truth, but it is not the *whole* truth. When he tells Demea

> With your assistance, therefore, Demea, I shall endeavour to defend what you justly call the adorable mysteriousness of the divine nature,

he gives to Demea less than a complete account of his view of Demea's position, and it is not until Part VII that poor Demea begins to feel that he is being left behind:

> Pray open up this argument a little farther, said Demea. For I do not rightly apprehend it, in that concise manner in which you have expressed it.

Eventually the penny drops:

> 'Hold! Hold!' cried Demea: 'Whither does your imagination hurry you? I joined alliance with you, in order to prove the incomprehensible nature of the divine Being, and refute the principles of Cleanthes, who would measure everything by a human rule and standard. But I now find you running into all the topics of the greatest libertines and infidels; and betraying that holy cause which you seemingly espoused. Are you secretly, then, a more dangerous enemy than Cleanthes himself?'

In a sense of course, Philo is, but the point I am stressing is his technique – assent and modification.

In Part XII precisely the same pattern operates. There are differences, but no significant ones. On the one hand the whole pattern is truncated and I shall return to this briefly: on the other he is dealing with a different, and one might say 'more reasonable' man in Cleanthes. Hence the modifications can emerge explicitly in discussion, for Cleanthes sees them coming quite clearly. Demea however, has no such perspicacity and suddenly finds himself overwhelmed by the difficulties in his position of which Cleanthes who had seen the writing on the wall, asks Demea,

> And are you so late in perceiving it?

My first point then is that any confession or affirmation of belief which Philo appears to make must be seen in context of a pattern of assent and modification already worked out in the *Dialogues*. The Philo who allows that

> A purpose, an intention, or design strikes everywhere the most careless and most stupid thinker . . .

allows little time for Cleanthes to feel the flush of success before he strips this apparent confession of faith of *most* of its meaning.

My second point, related closely to this is that for the first time Cleanthes and Philo are, so to speak, 'face to face'. Demea has gone. The significance of this can be seen by projecting the characters in the Dialogue back into Hume's own life. *Pace* Professors Pike and Capaldi, I do agree broadly with Kemp Smith, Mr

Gaskin and Professor Penelhum[5] that by and large Philo represents Hume's position. I do accept at face value his comment in the letter to Gilbert Elliot of Minto, quoted earlier. May I re-emphasize the final sentence of that quotation:

> I believe, too, we coud both òf us have kept our Temper very well.

This sentence is the nub of the point. Hume's friendship with the Moderates in the Church of Scotland is well established. His aversion to clerics was aversion to particular sorts of clerics and was quite compatible with his friendship with Hugh Blair, John Home, William Robertson etc. Cleanthes implicitly carries with him that element in Hume's life and it is not too far-fetched to see Demea as carrying with him the other side of the church conflict in Scotland, where dogmatism, of a much fiercer sort than Demea ever displays, attacked the Moderates by attacking Hume.

Only in Part XII is Philo prepared to argue as with an intimate, and to that extent he can let his intellectual hair down – 'a purpose . . . strikes everywhere – the most careless . . . thinker' – and indeed be *as far as he ever is and is capable of being*, honestly confessional:

> These, Cleanthes, are my unfeigned sentiments on this subject . . .

I do believe that through Philo in Part XII Hume was setting down his last word on the subject, as he might if his Moderate colleagues could persuade him to stop jesting on the subject.

This brings me to my third point: of course – and this is part of his approach to the matter – Philo did find it very difficult to establish the right tone for discussion. Pamphilus is accurate in characterizing Philo as proceeding in a manner 'somewhat between jest and earnest'. Further reference will be made to this point, but initially I offer it as one counter-example to the assumption that the Philo of Part XII is quite unannounced. The query raised in one's mind by this comment is one of a number of hints of what is to come. There is however another, which is much more striking, and which supports the biographical analogy which

I have been drawing. In Part III, Cleanthes replies to some of Philo's subtleties by asking Philo to 'come clean':

> Consider, anatomize the eye: Survey its structure and contrivance; and tell me *from your own feeling*, if the idea of a contriver does not *immediately flow in upon you with a force like that of sensation.*

This of course is the question which, so to speak, Philo answers positively in Part XII. Consider what Pamphilus tells us of his response in Part III:

> Here I could observe . . . that Philo was a little embarrassed and confounded: But while he hesitated in delivering an answer, luckily for him, Demea broke in upon the discourse, and saved his countenance.

Philo's discomfiture, I suggest, was not as Pamphilus implies, that he had lost the argument, but rather that it was not yet the right time, nor the right company to give a positive answer.

If we do find in Part XII Hume's own *credo* or testimony, then what is the content of that *credo*? His view is that if reasonable men who are intellectual neighbours in the borderlands between belief and unbelief consider the question carefully, they will come to see that the differences between them, believer and unbeliever, are less significant than might first appear. Indeed the sceptic Philo might even be prepared, given adequate qualifications, to accept the conclusion of 'natural theology'. The rub however, is that in so doing Hume is attempting to account for the *rational* or *intellectual* difference between believer and unbeliever as 'a species of controversy' which is 'merely verbal'. In order to evaluate the adequacy of such a conclusion, let us examine how Hume reaches it.

At the outset of the *Dialogues* we find Pamphilus, as in our earlier reference to him, coming near to but not quite grasping the truth. He stresses that for some subjects the dialogue form is appropriate. Such subjects include both those that we believe to be very familiar to us, and also those which are

... so *obscure* and *uncertain*, that human reason can reach no
fixed determination with regard to it; if it should be treated at
all; seems to lead us naturally into the style of dialogue and
conversation. Reasonable men may be allowed to differ, where
no one can reasonably be positive ...

Such a subject – both familiar and obscure – is Natural Religion.
Does this mean that the *Dialogues* can only provide, as Pamphilus
suggests, 'an agreeable amusement'? – with no real hope of outcome or conclusion? I think not. There is a conclusion and this
conclusion is to be found in a section of Part XII which picks up
this point from the Introduction. I believe that some concentration
on this under-rated theme and passage can help resolve some of the
residual uncertainties concerning the nature of Hume's conclusions.

My proposal is to concentrate on those sections of Part XII in
which Philo gives a rather clearer account of the obscurities and
uncertainties referred to earlier. At the beginning of the *Dialogues*
as Pamphilus and Cleanthes see it, the difference between belief
and unbelief is a difference about the empirical facts. This is, in
general, how both popular apologetics and natural theology presented the differences. The main thrust of the *Dialogues* is not to
affirm or deny the existence of God – again a matter on which we
are given guidance at the outset – but to establish what difference
there is between believing and not believing in such a God. As
Philo demonstrates to my satisfaction, the difference is not about
the inferences which may legitimately be drawn from the empirical facts – the uncertainties are of a different order.

... there is a species of controversy, which from the very nature
of language and of human ideas, is involved in perpetual
ambiguity, and can never, by any precaution or any definitions,
be able to reach a reasonable degree of precision.

The examples he offers initially concern 'degrees of any quality or
circumstance' e.g. the greatness of a man or the degree of Cleo-
patra's beauty. He continues,

That the dispute concerning theism is of this nature and consequently is merely verbal, or perhaps, if possible still, more

incurably ambiguous, will appear upon the slightest inquiry.

The conclusions of the *Dialogues* focus on this point. Hume has argued that philosophically speaking the difference between unbelief and the only acceptable form of belief is a dispute of words 'more than is usually imagined'.

There is comparison here between Hume's point and Wisdom's parable of the supernatural gardener.[6] In each case it is being stressed that the disagreement is not about empirical facts and inferences from them. There is however, one instructive point of difference. As the rest of Wisdom's paper *Gods* makes plain he is concerned to show that a great deal can hang on the use of one word – 'God' – rather than another. Hume leans in the other direction. Thus he wants to see the difference (as does Wisdom) as a matter of how the facts strike us and our verbal response. However his conclusion from this is that it does not matter whether we do use the word 'God' or not. This is because the sub-theme of Part X in particular, has limited the inferences to be drawn from the use of this word to all but the inconsequential. Let us reconsider a passage quoted earlier, but this time in its complete form.

If the whole of natural theology, as some people seem to maintain, resolves itself into one simple, though somewhat ambiguous, at least undefined proposition, *that the cause of or causes of order in the universe probably bear some remote analogy to human intelligence:* if this proposition be not capable of extension, variation, or more particular explication: if it afford no inference that affects human life, or can be the source of any action or forbearance: And if the analogy, imperfect as it is, can be carried no farther than to human intelligence, and cannot be transferred, with any appearance of probability, to the other qualities of the mind; if this really be the case, what can the most inquisitive, contemplative, and religious man do more than give a plain, philosophical assent to the proposition, as often as it occurs; and believe that the arguments, on which it is established, exceed the objections which lie against it?

The above comes from the penultimate paragraph of the *Dialogues* and precedes Philo's more oft quoted point about 'scepticism' being a prolegomena to 'sound, believing' Christianity. My proposal is that this is Philo's and Hume's 'last word' on the subject.

Philo is prepared to 'assent' to the relevant proposition which is simply a more careful formulation of his remark about what 'strikes the most careless . . .'. This is the only legitimate conclusion of 'natural theology' and he is prepared to agree with Cleanthes about it. As Demea earlier, so Cleanthes now may see that such agreement does not amount to much. Indeed if this is the conclusion that both he and Philo accept, then the dramatic change of belief in the *Dialogues* is to be found not in Philo, but in Cleanthes. The conclusion of Natural Theology, so significant for Cleanthes at the outset, is an anaemic matter indeed. Why should not Philo assent, for little hangs on it? – It is 'somewhat of a dispute about words'.

I have insisted that Hume did genuinely belong to the borderlands but I have reached the stage in my argument at which I must qualify this. He shared with his 'Moderate' friends a belief in the powers of rational discussion. He shared also an acceptance that what causes the religious sentiments in them may also be active in him:

> A purpose, an intention, a design strikes everywhere the most careless, the most stupid thinker; and no man can be so hardened in absurd systems, as at all times to reject it.

The *Philosophes* who would deny this are untrue to certain elements of their nature. Nonetheless whereas, as he remarked in the *Treatise*, the errors in philosophy are only ridiculous,

> Generally speaking, the errors in religion are dangerous.

He had adequate evidence of this in his own native land and I believe that his strategy in the *Dialogues* is directed towards showing and curtailing the dangers, discussed with great care in the *Natural History* and elsewhere, which arise through the exercise of 'natural' inclinations and propensities in the area of religion. Even the most intelligent and 'moderate' men were at risk here and the Cleanthes of this world had to be wooed with subtlety.

A crucial point in this is not to overstate one's case, and if, in all honesty, one does find certain aspects of the natural world striking in a particular way one should not completely discount this, even if one does carefully choose the moment to say so. Hume could never underestimate this form of immediacy and directness in one's experience, for it plays an absolutely central part in his account of what we, but not he, might call our moral beliefs. There is a parallel here and it is this. At the heart of his account of morality Hume placed the capacity of human beings to feel sentiments of praise or blame when confronted by certain situations. However, these sentiments were not *ipso facto* moral sentiments for one had to distinguish between the pleasurable feelings arising from contemplation of situations of personal advantage for example, and those which arise from the dispassionate contemplation of acts of kindness or benevolence. He sets out an account of how we can identify, encourage and safeguard such genuinely moral sentiments from other comparable feelings of pleasure and pain.[7]

In the case of religion he saw the dangers as much greater, and the tendency to corrupt much deeper. Consequently the safeguards – which he develops in the *Dialogues* – had to be much more thorough. Fortunately also, he did not believe religious sentiments, even in those limited contexts where they were tolerable, to be of much value and he was quite happy to consign them to the recreation-ground of experience. The real problem, of which he was well aware, was persuading others, even congenial spirits such as Cleanthes, to do likewise.

Conclusion

This study of David Hume shows the engagement of an intellectual with the nature and content of religious belief. He belongs to the borderlands where common presuppositions about the nature and direction of the discussion, even about our natural propensity for religious sentiments, are the basis for all enquiry. However, the outcome is not a blurring of the distinctions between belief and unbelief for in the end Hume has challenged the believer to establish that the dispute is not a mere verbal controversy. To meet such a challenge adequately the believer must show that despite the limitations of the intellect to which Hume's sceptical philosophy points, belief can be more than the thin verbal skin which Philo is willing to allow Cleanthes to attach to his experience of the world. Kierkegaard to whom we turn next can be seen as attempting to do precisely that.

3

SÖREN KIERKEGAARD

If David Hume seemed an unlikely tenant for the borderlands between belief and unbelief, so for quite contrary reasons does Sören Kierkegaard. Kierkegaard is for many the apostle of belief, he, it might well be argued, more than most, stands well clear of the border territory between belief and unbelief, for he of all the nineteenth-century writers on these matters speaks unambiguously in the accents of faith. As one who appears to place himself quite deliberately in the tradition of Abraham and Paul as interpreted by the Protestant Reformation, surely he has taken himself well beyond the concerns of lectures dealing with the borderlands occupied by the types of intellectual who are mercilessly pilloried in his writings. Yet this, I believe, is a distorted picture of Kierkegaard and to begin to re-align Kierkegaard's contribution to religious debate, let us heed the comment of Emil Brunner – no stranger himself to a firm Protestant emphasis upon faith:

> A Philosophy of Religion on a really noble scale, that thinks out modern problems in all seriousness; I mean, an attempt at an understanding between the Christian belief in revelation and the mind of our time is not to be found in that camp, with the single exception of *Sören Kierkegaard*.[1]

The context is a distinction drawn by Brunner between Kierkegaard and those other Protestant thinkers whose view of philosophy of religion fails to distinguish it from apologetics. Brunner is in this instance precisely but unfashionably correct in his insight into Kierkegaard's writings. Kierkegaard's personality, wit and style so distract us that it is easy to overlook the fact that he delivers the exposition of many of his most central ideas on the nature of Christianity and Christian faith to the pseudonymous author Johannes Climacus who refers to himself as 'an outsider'. Strange indeed that an author who is identified in the popular view with such phrases as 'the leap of faith' or 'faith is subjectivity', should write, so to speak, from the position of 'an outsider', for that is precisely what he does do in *Philosophical Fragments* and in the *Concluding Unscientific Postscript*.[2]

In addition to this there are certain correspondences between Kierkegaard and Hume which are far more important than their temperamental differences. Hume of course was even in his own terms 'a mitigated sceptic': Kierkegaard's infamous distrust of reason has philosophical roots in his appreciation of the sceptical tradition in Greek philosophy. In that respect it is closer to the refinement of Hume than to the gutteral tones of Luther. As with Hume, the preoccupation of much of Kierkegaard's work is with the limits of reason. His protest is not at reason and rationality *per se* but at the mistaken applications of certain specific patterns of reason within the area of religion. I am not proposing that there is any deep engagement in Kierkegaard with Hume's *Writings*, but there is a marked similarity of interests in a number of key areas. Thus his conclusions in *Philosophical Fragments* about the impossibility of arguing from the world to God are quite on a level with those of Hume in the *Dialogues*. His strictures on the limits of historical reasoning are again quite at one with Hume's naturalism in these matters. There are of course huge and substantial differences, but these arise from the exploration of common ground. Thus both Hume and Kierkegaard agree on the mistakenness of attempting to deduce moral laws from the nature of God. Hume's conclusion which as Capaldi correctly argues, is central to the whole enterprise of the *Dialogues*, is that religious belief should have no significance for human decision and action. Kierkegaard on the contrary believed that it should have ultimate significance for both – but *not* by being used as a foundation for morality.

The conclusion to Hume's scepticism was the insistence that the true difference between believer and unbeliever was merely verbal. Kierkegaard certainly could not agree with that, but his starting point shares with Hume not only scepticism with regard to the role of reason, but also the common ground that if there is a God then that God must be radically different from the finite anthropomorphic God of Cleanthes, whose nature may be inferred from his 'works'. At this point however, the common ground gives way to the sharper definition of the differences between belief and unbelief. The view which Philo is persuading Cleanthes to adopt is one which will involve Cleanthes in crossing the no-man's land from belief to unbelief. Kierkegaard's position would accept the untenability of Cleanthes' views but at the same time attempts to offer to the discussion a different account of the gap between belief and unbelief. Note however, how Kierkegaard sees his task in terms quite congenial to contemporary philosophy, namely,

> getting it made clear at least what Christianity is and where the confusions in Christendom lie.

As we shall see Kierkegaard's response is both complex and sophisticated.

There are two points which will be stressed initially in this presentation of Kierkegaard as a man of the borderlands. On the one hand it is important to see that in Humean terms Kierkegaard's response to scepticism is to argue that the dispute between belief and unbelief is seen as merely verbal controversy in so far as we restrict ourselves to what can be directly communicated. On the other hand to communicate indirectly is in part to develop a whole style of writing and arguing which will depend, amongst other things, on the use of the pseudonyms already mentioned. As such it is certainly, I shall argue, to belong to the borderlands. However in order to justify such a contentious conclusion I shall have to attempt the impossible, namely to give an exposition of Kierkegaard's thought: the first problem to be encountered is that of how to write about Kierkegaard for it would be easy in the attempt to summarize, to use direct forms of communication where Kierkegaard has shown their inadequacy.

I

One could write as a disciple and enthuse about this or that – about the wit, about the originality, about the style, or about the way in which one's own 'insights' are prefigured here and there in Kierkegaard's most inspired moments. If however, one is moderately well read in the major works, one might avoid that particular snare and congratulate oneself on recalling the acidic reflections of the pseudonymous author of the *Concluding Unscientific Postscript*, Johannes Climacus, on the topic of discipleship:

> Even if I strove with might and main to become Lessing's disciple, I could not, for Lessing has prevented it. Just as he himself is free, so I imagine that he desires to make everyone else free in relation to himself. He begs to be excused the exhalations and gaucheries of the disciple, fearing to be made ridiculous through repetitioners who reproduce what is said like a prattling echo.[3]

The alternative would seem to be critical, scholarly exposition and analysis – by stating directly and unequivocally what Kierkegaard thought about God, man and Christ, the truth about whom Kierkegaard believed could only be communicated indirectly – by being objective and dispassionate about what was, for Kierkegaard, a matter for passion and inwardness – by placing historically his remarks about what is of eternal significance – by becoming that 'remarkable species of animal', 'a town crier of inwardness'.

Perhaps those whose response to the above is not positive, can at least sympathise with the predicament. It is part of the predicament of Johannes Climacus vis-à-vis Lessing:

> If I were to set about expounding the several ideas, patteringly referring them to him directly, dutifully enclosing him in my admiring embrace as one to whom I owed everything, he would perhaps smilingly withdraw, leaving me in the lurch, an object of ridicule.[4]

Although in his otherwise appropriate and sympathetic introduction to *The Present Age*[5] Walter Kaufmann goes further than I can accept in suggesting that Kierkegaard was a misanthropist, there is no doubt that Kierkegaard savoured in anticipation the humour in the interpreter's predicament.

How then are we to proceed, or may we not proceed at all? Initially at least we have sniffed at some of the dangers, and the image of a suspicious dog is no bad one to keep in mind as we approach Kierkegaard's writings, for things with Kierkegaard are not always as they seem. This has led to a number of myths growing up around the figure and thought of Kierkegaard – myths which intelligent laymen and students absorb from the proliferation of general accounts of the sort which you are now reading, and failing that, from the comments of philosophers, theologians and clerics who may have read such an introduction. Minimally one can hope to achieve something by counterbalancing the bias of these impressions.

Perhaps the distortion most easily corrected is the picture of Kierkegaard the gloomy humourless Dane. Certainly Kierkegaard deals with issues which are serious, perhaps to the extent of appearing depressingly sombre, but as for Plato the human activity nearest to the contemplation of what is ultimate is the study of mathematics, so for Kierkegaard the penultimate is humour – and there is no implication that the ultimate discards the penultimate. His own writings are generously laced with wit, be it in description of his own generation, in vignettes of the absurdities which bedevil the sermonizer, or in his question of the 'unworldly' philosopher:

> Is he himself *sub specie aeterni*, even when he sleeps, eats, blows his nose, or whatever else a human being does?[6]

Whatever is the truth of the matter, it is not to be found in the view of Kierkegaard as humourless, and if we do not learn from Kierkegaard when to smile at our own human follies, then he has little to teach us.

A more subtle variation on the theme of Kierkegaard the gloomy Dane, is to be found in the suggestion that the degree of originality in Kierkegaard's work corresponds to the level of the disturbance of his psyche. At a crude level this amounts to the 'genetic fallacy' of discounting the value of something because of some beliefs about the unworthiness of its origins. However, one need not be as explicit as this, in order to cast doubts upon the credibility of a writer, and it is undoubtedly true that Kierkegaard was a highly distinctive individual. He often refers to his unusually severe religious upbringing and describes it as 'humanly speaking – crazy'[7] and the contrast between his outward mode of existence, a wit and party-goer, apparently happy to fritter away his time in strolling the streets and conversing with all and sundry, and his inner suffering and self-denial, is to say the least, unusual. He suggests that,

> Only the man who knows in his own experience what true self-denial is can solve my riddle and perceive that it is self-denial. For the man who in himself has no experience of it must rather call my behaviour self-love, pride, eccentricity, madness . . .[8]

And indeed there are many who are prepared to hazard opinions as to Kierkegaard's mental health. For example G. E. and G. B. Arbaugh quote Geisman's view that Kierkegaard is 'a completely untypical form of manic-depressive', and offer the alternative interpretation that he is a 'maladjusted neurotic, but certainly not psychotic'.[9] Kierkegaard was himself aware of the precariousness of his own psychological equilibrium, but he believed that this was the consequence rather than the cause of his understanding of the way the world is, and he was in retrospective reflection, quite explicit about the significance of his belief in God in relation to this. He talks of himself as 'alone in dialectical tensions which (without God) would drive any man with my imagination to madness.'[10] He would want to insist, however, that there is an internal relationship between such psychological states and man's awareness of his relationship to God, rather than that belief in such a relationship to God is caused by certain psychological needs. Further discussion of this point must await discussion of the understanding of the nature of belief in God which he outlines in his writings.

The third Kierkegaardian myth, which I shall only mention at this point, for detailed consideration will be given to the issues concerned in due course, is that there are three different and dis-

crete stages or types of human life, the aesthetic, the ethical and
the religious. It is not a mistake to suggest that there are three different types or stages of life discussed by Kierkegaard, but it is a
gross error to suggest that the three different stages, or forms of
life are so discrete that the aesthetic and the ethical play no part at
all in the religious. The origins of this myth may well lie in a
limited acquaintance with two of Kierkegaard's earliest publications: *Either/Or* and *Fear and Trembling*.[11] In the former of these
the choice which seems to be implied in the title can be read as an
exclusive choice between the life of the alleged but anonymous
author of the papers in volume one, simply referred to as 'A', and
the advice of the reflective judge given to A in volume two: an
exclusive choice, that is to say, between sophisticated aestheticism
and duty-conscious morality. In *Fear and Trembling*, the author
Johannes de Silentio, stresses the disjunction between the ethical
and the religious. In his discussion of Abraham and his prepared-
ness to sacrifice Isaac, a contrast is delineated between the universal
demands of morality and the religious duty to sacrifice his son
apparently demanded by God of Abraham: here the religious
transcends the ethical, and what is, from the point of view of the
ethical, murder, is, religiously regarded, an absolute duty.

The myth that erects exclusive barriers between the aesthetic,
the ethical and the religious is misleading in two main ways: on
the one hand it undervalues the significance of the points of
transition between the three 'stages', at the expense of the much
over-emphasized metaphor of 'the leap' to which Kierkegaard
occasionally resorts; on the other hand it encourages forgetfulness
of the fact that dialectic not only plays a role within specific writings, but also, as Kierkegaard himself came later to suggest, that it
plays a role *between* one work and another.[12] That is to say, no *one*
work, particularly amongst the earlier writings, should be seen as
presenting the whole story or as offering a complete statement of
Kierkegaard's view of any issue.

The questions which follow from this are crucial in any attempt
to understand Kierkegaard's writings: Why are these dangers inherent in reading Kierkegaard? Why is it that as one work may
illuminate, so it may also mislead? Is it perhaps perversity on the

part of the author? Is it, alternatively, simply that as with other writers, Kierkegaard's views changed so that we find the early Kierkegaard, and the later Kierkegaard, with perhaps the hint of a middle period to be excised from the corpus by a discerning PhD candidate? That there was development and therefore change is true, but the historical charting of the movements of emphases involved is a less important aid to understanding Kierkegaard, than is a consideration of the methods employed by Kierkegaard in his writing. The methods which he employed, including the structure and style of individual works, were dictated by the subject-matter of those works, and, as he came later to argue[13] by a strategy which became increasingly conscious in his literary activities.

The difficulties then, in writing about, in reading, and in attempting to understand Kierkegaard are considerable. The dangers of overstatement and simplification lurk constantly in the wings but in an initial survey of some of the problems facing the student of Kierkegaard, at least some progress has been made, and a tentative answer to the question 'How to proceed?' has emerged. Avoidance of the third of the 'myths' outlined above, it has been suggested, rests, amongst other things, upon an adequate appreciation of the methods which structured Kierkegaard's writings individually and collectively. The importance of this for Kierkegaard goes far beyond the appreciation of mere complexity of structure and finesse of style, for Kierkegaard's own sensitivity to method and style stems from his own appropriation[14] of the subject matter in question – the life of faith and its implications for the nature of human existence. Hence, Kierkegaard's writings embody a view later to become central in Karl Barth's thinking, that while method is of fundamental importance in theology and philosophy, method is subordinate to subject-matter. The converse of this, however, which is to be the guiding principle in what follows, is that for a writer such as Kierkegaard or Barth while method is not prior *in ordine essendi*, it may well be prior *in ordine cognoscendi*.

A further benefit to be derived from such an approach is that while, as we saw, Kierkegaard warns plainly of the dangers of trying to be objective and dispassionate about what is for him a

matter of passion and inwardness, and of the impossibility of stating directly what he believed could be communicated only indirectly, he nowhere forbids discussion of his work at a second
remove, *via* that is, discussion of the methods which he employed.
Indeed, two of his works in particular, are largely concerned with
precisely that – *Concluding Unscientific Postscript* and *The Point of
view of My Work as Author*. Each of these holds a peculiarly significant place in the Kierkegaard *corpus*; the former being the first
major publication (1846) to which he attaches his own name,
albeit as editor, and in which he admits authorial responsibility for
the earlier pseudonymous works;[15] the latter written in 1848 and
published posthumously can be read as Kierkegaard's own recognition that his writings to that point could be considered as
ambiguous, and hence liable to misunderstanding. In the light of
this, much of the subsequent discussion will focus upon the significance of these two works.

II

One of the most striking and initially most puzzling features of
Kierkegaard's writings is his liberal use of pseudonyms and
'editors'. The particular pseudonyms selected have significance in
themselves, e.g. Victor Eremit the name given to the 'editor' of
Either/Or signifies one who has been 'victorious' or 'successful' in
the solitary life of the religious recluse. More generally Kierkegaard gives a retrospective account or explanation of this practice
in *The Point of View*. There he divides his writings up to that point
(1848) into the religious and the aesthetic, with *Concluding Unscientific Postscript* occupying a pivotal or bridging position. The
aesthetic group then comprised *Either/Or, Fear and Trembling,
Repetition, The Concept of Dread, Prefaces, Philosophical Fragments*,
and *Stages on Life's Way*; the religious group included *Edifying
Discourses* (several), *Works of Love*, and *Christian Discourses*.
   The aesthetic works were all pseudonymous, and were very
largely published before *Concluding Unscientific Postscript*. The
religious works published under Kierkegaard's own name largely
belong to the later period. The *Postscript*, as was noted earlier was

published under the pseudonym of Johannes Climacus, but with Kierkegaard's own name appearing on the title page as 'responsible for publication'. To the chronological grouping there are exceptions which Kierkegaard counted as of particular importance, e.g. the religious work *Two Edifying Discourses* was published in the same year as *Either/Or* (1843) and the aesthetic article *The Crisis and a Crisis in the Life of an Actress* was published in the midst of a stream of religious writings in 1848.

The significance of these two works is that Kierkegaard's retrospective account of his publications insists that the two streams, aesthetic and religious, had each been present throughout his activity as a writer. Most particularly he rejected the idea that he was an aesthete who in the course of time had abandoned the aesthetic for the religious. He wished his work to be understood as a unity with a dialectic at play between the different writings and groups of writings. There are, however, two qualifications which must be made here: on the one hand it is in general terms unlikely that he had from the outset a complete grasp of the questions tackled in *Concluding Unscientific Postscript*, if only because there he mounts a concerted attack on Hegelianism which goes well beyond any previous and less unsympathetic views of Hegel's writings; on the other hand Kierkegaard does admit that the account he gives is retrospective and that it would not be wholly true to claim 'that from the very first instant I had a survey of the whole authorship'.[16] Nonetheless he does insist upon unity in his published work.

The basis for the unity is that each of the works in its own way confronts what Johannes Climacus refers to in the Introduction to the *Postscript* as 'the problem'. The problem can take a variety of forms, but the one which Kierkegaard sees his authorship as confronting, he calls 'the subjective problem' of 'the relationship of the individual to Christianity' which is the focus of the second and larger part of the Postscript. It must be remembered, however, that the Postscript is the work of Johannes Climacus, who styles himself as 'an outsider' to Christianity who has, nonetheless 'understood at least so much, that the only unpardonable offense against the majesty of Christianity is for the individual to take his relationship to it for granted, treating it as a matter of course.' That this level of understanding is possible for an outsider is crucial to Kierkegaard's method and ignorance of this led to the name of Kierkegaard being introduced in a confused and confusing manner into contemporary discussions of whether faith precedes understanding or vice-versa. It has been too recently assumed that Kierkegaard's occasional appeal to the metaphor of the leap of faith has put him unequivocally amongst those who affirm in a radical sense that until the lamp of faith has been lit by some form of divine encounter or experience, then all is darkness and understanding is impossible. Whatever else it amounts to, Kierkegaard's talk of subjectivity cannot be equated with that form of simplistic epistemological subterfuge.

Kierkegaard's whole strategy points to the falseness of this interpretation, as becomes particularly apparent in his account of the use of pseudonyms for the aesthetic writings. The unity in his writings is the unity given by Kierkegaard in his insistence that even if it is too strong to claim that he was always dedicated 'to defend Christianity', unswervingly, his intention has been 'to present it (Christianity) in its true form'. He also tells us with exemplary philosophical intent that his 'expression of a melancholy love for men', was to bring about 'above all clearness of thinking, and that especially about Christianity'. Indeed he confesses that from a time predating his published works he had resolved

> even if I were never to attain the goal of becoming a Christian, I would employ all my time and diligence to getting it made clear at least what Christianity is and where the confusions in Christendom lie.

The point here is that Kierkegaard thought it quite possible to fulfil this resolve, independently of his own subjective relation to Christianity. Not only may the non-believer come to an understanding of what Christianity is, he can help others to do so as well. Hence, Kierkegaard found no methodological problems in carrying out this task through the medium of pseudonymous aesthetic writings – writings that is, emanating from the standpoint of the aesthetic rather than the religious.

Apart from this point, which has important philosophical implications, Kierkegaard believed that there were other benefits to be
derived from the role of 'deceit' which he adopted in the pseudonymous aesthetic works. His age, he believed was one which
was under an illusion: the age had lost all sense of what it was to
become a Christian. The notion of being an individual had been
submerged in the idea of 'the public' –

the abstract whole formed in the most ludicrous way, by all
participants becoming a third party (an onlooker).[17]

Completely absent was the realization that true community presupposes that the individuals who belong to it have acquired an
ethical outlook.[18] Hence, much of his finest polemical comment is
reserved for those who by appealing to size or numbers obscure
the responsibility of the individual for his own relationship to be
eternal. His contemporaries, he believed, were also particularly
prone to substitute intellectuality and 'philosophy' for passion and
paradox. The result of this was the tacit belief that one could be
Christian 'up to a point', and that the assimilation or appropriation of Christianity was a comparatively simple and easy matter.
Faith it seems, provides no difficulties either in understanding what
it is, or in realizing it.

In those old days it was different, then faith was a task for a
whole lifetime.[19]

whereas now,

It is supposed to be difficult to understand Hegel, but to understand Abraham is a trifle. To go beyond Hegel is a miracle, but
to get beyond Abraham is the easiest thing of all.[20]

Kierkegaard's justification of what from one point of view looks
like the 'deception' of using pseudonyms rests upon his understanding of what it is to dispel illusions as deep as these. What is
bound to fail, he thought, is the stance of the preacher, the sermonizer, the committed enthusiast:

No, an illusion can never be destroyed directly, and only by indirect means can it be radically removed. If it is an illusion, that all are Christians – and if there is anything to be done about it, it must be done indirectly, not by one who vociferously proclaims himself an extraordinary Christian, but by one who, better instructed, is ready to declare that he is not a Christian.[21]

To assume that one can communicate directly to the man under an illusion as to the nature of Christianity, is to make a simple but far-reaching error about the situation confronting one:

> Whoever rejects this opinion betrays that he is not overwell versed in dialectics, and that is precisely what is needed when operating in this field. For there is an immense difference, a dialectical difference, between these two cases ... direct communication presupposes that the receiver's ability to receive is undisturbed. But here such is not the case; an illusion stands in the way.[22]

Removal of the illusion demands indirect communication – communication, that is, from the standpoint of the aesthetic. As noted already this contains the implicit assumption that the truth about Christianity can be communicated and *a fortiori* can be understood by the non-believer. Also implicit here, is one of the most striking and consistent notes sounded throughout Kierkegaard's writing.

Always, if the communication concerns man's eternal happiness we deal only with the individual. For Kierkegaard an individual, a human being, is never a one-sided abstraction; to communicate is thus never to address simply the individual's intellect; it is never simply a matter of offering a series of well-structured arguments, be they inductive or deductive. Nor on the other hand is communication with an individual ever simply a matter of effecting an emotional response: oratory is no satisfactory alternative either. In each case to address the one without the other, intellect without the emotions, or the heart independently of the head, is to attempt to communicate with a less-than-complete individual, and one of the lessons least learnt or most commonly mislearned from Kierkegaard by later generations, is his conception of what it is to be an individual human being – an integrated and complete self. The chief danger of his own age, he believed, was the danger of becoming an age without passion, a reflective age in which

> Equally unthinkable among the young men of today is a truly religious renunciation of the world, adhered to with daily self-denial.[23]

Perhaps in our own day the chief danger is an un-Kierkegaardian subjectivity in which a relativizing of all judgment discredits and discards the careful analyses of human character and personality which we find in Kierkegaard.

Kierkegaard's use of the pseudonyms also brings to light a surprising and indeed paradoxical feature of Kierkegaard's thought which helps delineate further his concept of subjectivity. Although he is rightly regarded as the apostle of subjectivity, passion, and engagement, in the writings as a whole, and in the aesthetic writings in particular, his method is not the direct communication of the enthusiast, the engaged or the committed man as the twentieth century understands these terms. Instead of cogent and persuasive apologetics, instead of impassioned exhortation, he seems almost to detach himself from his beliefs, to hold them, so to speak at arm's length. Thus, it would be difficult to gather from the aesthetic writings, or even from *Concluding Unscientific Postscript* what the relationship of the author is to Christianity, and indeed Johannes Climacus disavows any suggestion that he is himself a believer. That is to say that Kierkegaard entrusts to the pen of a non-believer his most important insights on the nature of religion in general and Christianity in particular. This in itself underlines what Kierkegaard regarded as the greatest need of his day: 'above all clearness of thinking, and that especially about Christianity'. It also raises the question of the role of such notions as 'hiddenness' and 'the incognito' in Kierkegaard's account of subjectivity, and to this we must shortly turn.

To summarize then, in his use of pseudonyms we can trace three different strands at work. Initially it is a device, and this part of his method is dictated not by subject-matter but by human psychology. This is based upon his insistence that communication to men suffering under an illusion must be rather different from the direct communication of truths to the acceptance of which there are no inner impediments. Secondly, however, the nature of what is to be communicated is such that one cannot simply by formal argument, or enthusiastic exhortation, bring men to the point of agreement or acceptance. The 'appropriation' of Christianity must, because of what faith is, be a solitary or individual matter. The most that written communication can do is to clarify the individual's thinking about what Christianity is. Such a task – clarification – does not presuppose faith or belief on the part of the communicator and thus is an eminently suitable subject for the writer of an 'aesthetic' work. Finally, a point which has emerged, and which is the subject of extended discussion in the *Postscript*, is that the use of pseudonyms is consonant with, even illustrative of, Kierkegaard's view that since faith is a matter of an individual's inner life, the hidden-ness of faith seems at times compatible with, and at other times almost to demand, an outer appearance not discriminably different from that of unbelief.

One footnote must be added to our discussion of *The Point of View*. Although Kierkegaard does at times talk as if the writings were all composed according to one grand design, elsewhere he moderates his tone:

> For in case I were to affirm out and out that from the first instant I had a survey of the whole authorship; or that at every moment, stage by stage, I had by anticipation so far exhausted the possibilities that later reflection had not taught me anything, not even this other thing, that though what I had done was surely right, yet only afterwards was I in a position to understand thoroughly that this was so – if I were to do this, it would be a denial of God and dishonesty towards Him.[24]

Kierkegaard clearly has in mind here 'the share of Governance . . . in the authorship', and he is presenting us with a picture of the authorship as exemplifying the Pauline exhortation which he used as a title for his book on Abraham: 'Work out your own salvation with fear and trembling, for it is God which worketh in you.' For our purposes, however, the significance of the remark is that Kierkegaard's view of his work as an author was a view that *developed*. What he tells us of *Either/Or* or *Fear and Trembling* in 1848 is not necessarily what, if we could have prevailed on him, he would have told us of these books in 1843. Nonetheless this does not invalidate the later remarks as a source of understanding these two books, especially if our intention is to come to some understanding of the authorship as a whole.

III

Kierkegaard is sometimes referred to as the father of existentialism. The mistake implicit in this metaphorical assertion is the assumption that there is some one thing called existentialism seeking parentage. Certainly many of the themes discussed by Kierkegaard have been taken up subsequently by writers who are referred to as existentialists. A theme of crucial importance here is the nature of human existence: what is it to be a human being? As Kant did before him . . . so Kierkegaard emphasized the way in which temporality is unavoidably part of the texture of human life. For Kant what this amounted to was a belief that all human experience is temporally conditioned: we perceive, we think we feel, always in time. Kierkegaard treats this point essentially in ethical terms, and relates man's temporality to his fulfilment or happiness. The connection he makes is this: so inevitable is the temporality of human life, that one must conceive of human existence as a process of movement. In this sense to be finite is to be always in a state of becoming, never in a stage of final completion or fulfilment. To be finite is to be temporal: to be temporal is to be constantly in a state of change or movement; to be constantly in a state of movement is to be less than wholly complete or fulfilled, it is to have less than eternal happiness.

What these abstractions add up to for the individual is that the individual can never decide as the rich man of the parable decided to say to himself:

> Soul, thou hast much goods laid up for many years, take thine ease.

For to think in that way is to fall under the illusion that there is a final fulfilled state of rest open to the human being which can be achieved by endeavour, good luck, skill, or any other means. Eternal happiness cannot in this way be possessed in time, for eternal happiness is man's absolute telos, his final fulfilment. But if the mark of the existing individual is that he is always 'in the process of becoming', and if 'in existence the watchword is always forward,'[25] then there can be for the existing individual no state of rest or completion.

If these minimal claims about what it is to be an existing individual, are granted, then Kierkegaard's method in the *Concluding Unscientific Postscript* is to raise the question of what the significance of these claims is for what it is to be a Christian. As Johannes Climacus continually stresses, this is not to raise the question of the objective truth of Christianity, but is rather in the nature of a thought experiment. There is much in this that prefigures the concentration of many twentieth-century theologians upon the significance for Christian theology of the acceptance of this or that philosophical analysis of the nature of human existence. A particularly striking contemporary example of this is Rudolf Bultmann's appeal to Heidegger's analysis of existence. Kierkegaard's analysis, however, is different from that of Heidegger's as his practice is different from that of Bultmann's.

From the above minimal claims about individual existence Kierkegaard extends his analysis by insisting upon the importance of the ethical in our understanding of human beings. Two remarks show unambiguously how important this is: he complains of Hegelian philosophy that it lacks 'an Ethics (where existence properly belongs)';[26] and in emphasizing the significance of the ethical for the individual, he indicates two ways in which this is the case:

> Ethics and the ethical, as constituting the essential anchorage for all individual existence, have an indefeasible claim upon every existing individual.[27]

The second point, the indefeasible claim of the ethical is very much a part of Kierkegaard's Kantian legacy; the first point also reflects a Kantian doctrine, but less directly and clearly. Kant's way of putting the point is that for a human being to possess the quality of rationality is to recognize and impose upon himself the universal moral law. Kierkegaard's way of asserting a crucial point about the relationship between the ethical and the nature of human existence is to argue that there are at least two different ways of, or kinds of existence, there is the existence of the subject who avoids or ignores his own ethical reality, who recognizes no transcendent claim upon himself, and there is the existence of 'a genuine human being' who,

> as a synthesis of the finite and the infinite, finds his reality in holding these two factors together, infinitely interested in existing.[28]

Or, as he tells a little later in the same book,

> The real subject is the ethically existing subject.[29]

Kierkegaard's use of the contentious terms 'genuine' and 'real' may distract attention from the central point being made. He is rejecting any conception of human fulfilment or significance being found only in discovering the place of the human being within the framework of some universal historical process. A man who holds such a view seeks in the end what Kierkegaard calls 'world-historical significance'. The problems in sustaining such an aim are twofold; on the one hand there is no guarantee of success,

> Neither by willing the good with all his strength, nor by satanic obduracy in willing what is evil, can a human being be assured of historical significance.[30]

Even the greatest figures upon the world-historical scene depend upon the accidental and the contingent: for the want of a horse-shoe-nail or a transistor a battle *could* be lost. On the other hand the endemic uncertainty of achieving significance in one's influence upon historical change, provides the greatest temptation – a preoccupation with the world-historical, with achieving results that can be quantitatively measured, 'instead of concerning themselves solely with the essential, the inner spirit, the ethical, freedom'. Whatever else is true of Kierkegaard, he is certainly not a utilitarian. He is not opposed to the achievement of results, the relief of suffering, and so on, but he sees the appeal to these as either the criterion, or as the constituents of ethical action, as wholly misguided, and as ethically dangerous.

The discussion of this is, as we must remind ourselves, set within the context of an enquiry by Johannes Climacus into what it amounts to be a believer. The rejection of 'results' or 'effects' as irrelevant is a consequence of two facts. The first is that if it promises anything, Christianity promises eternal happiness, complete fulfilment; the second is that the pursuit of this in the world-historical terms of significance or fulfilment found in bringing about changes of a historical nature, changes in the spatio-temporal world, carries no guarantee of success. To attempt to define human fulfilment in world-historical terms is to attempt to find eternal unchanging significance or purpose in a temporal, and therefore ever-changing context,

> – and this is impossible because it is merely possible, i.e. perhaps possible, i.e. dependent upon something else.[31]

Two main features of Kierkegaard's account of what it is to be a human being have emerged; it is to be a temporal creature, never at rest; it is to be denied the seemingly obvious route to the eternal happiness and fulfilment promised by Christianity, i.e. the route through 'works', through bringing about results which are external to oneself. Two related consequences follow from this: *if* there is the possibility of reflecting eternity in one's life (and one must remember that for Johannes Climacus this was always an hypothesis), this can only be in that area of life where the achievement of external results is *not* decisive, not the criterion of fulfilment, that is to say in the area of one's willing and one's deciding, in Kierkegaard's terms, in 'becoming subjective'. As a second consequence Kierkegaard argued that in these matters it is the manner in which the individual apprehends or appropriates the truth about his own finitude which is decisive: not what it is that he apprehends, but the way in which he apprehends it. The point here is not, as it is sometimes twisted to be, that it does not matter what you believe as long as you believe it in some ultimately committed way: it is rather that the 'what' of belief, which can be

communicated directly, or objectively, is not a necessary and sufficient condition of faith, though this does not rule out the possibility that in times different from his own, it might have to be
stressed that the 'what' of belief is a *necessary* condition of faith
correctly called Christian.[32]

Before drawing out the significance of this for the way in which
Kierkegaard believed truth might be communicated, it will be of
value to note some of Kierkegaard's remarks about the relationship between God and man. He talks in a way followed by Barth
in his *Epistle to the Romans*, of 'an absolute difference' between
God and man. God is infinite and eternal while man 'although
eternal' is essentially 'a particular existing being'. If this is the case,
then no approach can be made to God through speculative argument, or through appeal to evidence of God's existence in nature.
Such argument can neither *prove* that God exists,[33] nor show what
is the nature of God as an object, knowledge of which could be
approximate, or 'up to a point', and whose existence would be
like the existence of other objects, i.e. in space and time. God,
however, he tells us in a rather difficult remark,

> is a subject, and therefore exists only for subjectivity in inward-
> ness.[34]

This remark is perhaps clearer in what it denies than in what it
affirms.

It denies, for example, that one can make non-misleading
affirmations about the nature of God. It denies also that one can
have an 'immediate' relationship with God, for that, he claims, is
paganism. Thus his conception of God is not such that one can
strike bargains with him, or ask questions of him, or even temporarily believe oneself to have satisfied the demands he may make
of a believer. Any conception of God which allows such directness in one's dealings with him forgets the absolute difference
which there is between God and man. Consequently there is no
direct expression of a man's relationship to God. As God is elusive
or hidden from direct awareness, so man's relationship to God is
elusive and secret and lacks direct expression. Not even the monas-
tic life of the cloister is adequate as an expression of man's devotion

to God because even there one makes the mistake of 'coming to rest' in the belief that one has found a way of life which is externally distinctive and which is a full or adequate expression of a relationship to God. If, however, the nature of God is to be hidden, and the only adequate relation to that God is indirect and inward, then the expression of that relationship must itself be indirect and inward. This is why Kierkegaard writes with respect to individual man,

> A direct relationship between one spiritual being and another, with respect to essential truth, is unthinkable. If such a relationship is assumed, it means that one of the parties has ceased to be spirit.[35]

This does not deny that there are direct relationships between existing individuals for all world-historical relationships are direct: what it denies is that these have anything to do with 'essential truth'.

We have seen then that both because of the nature of human existence, temporal, continually changing, and yet a synthesis of finite and infinite, and because of the nature of God eternal, hidden, and absolutely different, the pattern of communication between man and man, and the relationship of the individual to God will require careful elucidation. Of relationship to God, the absolute good, Kierkegaard tells us,

> an eternal happiness as the absolute good has the remarkable trait of *being definable solely in terms of the mode of acquisition*.[36]

The grounds for this claim are to be founded in the two correlated claims about God, that he is 'absolutely different' and that his existence and his presence are hidden. A consequence of this is that for subjectivity, the question of truth is the question of whether or not the individual is related to something '*in such a manner* that his relationship is in truth a God-relationship', whereas for objectivity, the question had always been whether the object of any such relationship is 'the true God'.[37] The importance of this move cannot be under-estimated. Taken at its most radical and this has often been its influence, what is involved is the substitution of the mechanism or psychology of faith, for the object of faith as the focus of theological and philosophical discussion.

In Kierkegaard's defence against such a radical interpretation three points can be made. First, although Kierkegaard did 'emphasize' the manner of acceptance of a truth, he did not *substitute* this for the truth. This was part of the dialogue which he carried on with his contemporaries. Secondly Kierkegaard's thought and writing is dominated, one might even say 'domineered', throughout by the conception of a transcendent and sovereign God, in a way that for example, Bultmann's is not. Whereas much of Bultmann's emphasis upon the act and moment of faith seems to derive directly from his understanding of the way things are with modern man, for Kierkegaard the emphasis upon mode of acquisition is a consequence of a conception of an absolutely transcendent God and of a view, not of what modern man can or cannot believe, but of the enduring character of human existence. Thirdly, in the end Kierkegaard did not view either God, or the God-relationship, as a matter for theological or any other form of 'discussion', as is clear from his account of 'indirect communication' (the topic to which we must now turn, having noted the dangers of selecting, one aspect of Kierkegaard's thought and treating it as a doctrine abstractable from a systematic theology or the like).

Kierkegaard characterizes the difference between direct and indirect communication by means of his discussion of 'double reflection'. 'The form of a communication', he tells us, 'must be distinguished from its expression'. By 'the expression' of a communication, I take Kierkegaard to mean its expression in words. This is what is realized 'by means of a first reflection'. The second reflection concerns the relationship between the author of the communication and the communication. If the communication is of some factual belief concerning the truth of which we have some doubt, then the belief in question plus our relationship (here = attitude) to it can be communicated directly thus: 'I am not certain that we have enough petrol to reach the next service station.' If, however, the communication concerns what is of existential import to us, i.e. concerns our absolute *telos,* our eternal happiness or fulfilment, then various differences must be noted. The relationship in question is an inward or subjective relationship. It is of absolute importance, yet because our existence is temporal and changing there is no fixed form by which its direct expression can be modified to show this absolute or over-riding importance. Notwithstanding, any communication of the truth in question, must, if it is to be adequate, communicate precisely this, for it must communicate not just the truth in question (e.g. 'truth is subjectivity') but also the significance and nature of the mode of acquisition of this truth. Appropriation of the truth which edifies cannot be a matter for group acquisition, like the queue of bare arms and rumps in a mass immunization campaign. The truth which edifies can only be appropriated by the existing individual for himself, and this too must be communicated.

How is this possible? How can we communicate what is essentially inward, momentary and hidden? The answer is that one cannot. The most one can do is show that this is a possibility, and at the same time attempt to cancel the dangers and illusions of direct and over-reaching communication. Hence the use of pseudonyms and the holding of belief and conviction at arm's length; hence the use of irony to mark the limits of the aesthetic and the point of transition from the aesthetic to the ethical; hence the use of the comic to mark the limits of the ethical and its transition to the religious; hence also the use of dialectic within his works and between them.

The aim of communication is, within this context, to bring about deeper knowledge and understanding in the hearer. However, such deeper knowledge of what is of ultimate concern or importance cannot be wholly communicated between persons. Certain truths can only be appropriated or grasped individually and inwardly, and the communication of *these* truths must somehow mark this fact about them. Thus a man who wishes to communicate to others what the nature of his religious belief is must communicate not only what these beliefs are, but *how he* is related to them. Now his relationship to these beliefs is individual and inward. To attempt to communicate directly what is the nature of his belief in the forgiveness of God is *ipso facto* to make it a matter of what is public and external; that is to say his relationship to these beliefs cannot be made a matter of direct communication for this would be to change the character of the relationship, and would thus fail to communicate what that relationship is. It would also violate the 'secrecy' which Kierkegaard believed essential to it.

Kierkegaard believed that secrecy was essential here for three correlated reasons. One is, as we have already noted, that God, because he is absolutely different, must remain hidden or incognito, for, there is no adequate means of representing directly and positively what he is like. The second reason for secrecy is that because the individual is both temporal and always in a state of becoming, there is no final expression of the individual's relationship to the eternal which can serve as a resting place for the understanding. The third reason is that if direct communication were attempted then there would be a danger that the personality of the communicator would become so linked to the truth in question, that it might constitute 'a danger to both the communicator and the hearer in being a distraction from inwardness. It is for this last reason that Kierkegaard had little desire to acquire disciples.

IV

There are certain corollaries of the issues discussed in the previous section, which we are now in a position to eludicate further.

According to Kierkegaard, direct communication often presupposes a certainty about what is communicated. This is true whether or not we are communicating a doubt in our own mind, such as the witness who answers, 'I am not sure whether it was the vicar who shouted "Down with the Fuzz!" ' or a fact of which we are quite certain, e.g. 'Mr. Jones lives in the house with the blue door'. Direct communication presupposes also a finality about what is communicated: that is to say, it presupposes that one has, or has grasped, a truth to communicate, and that this truth is expressible in terms of a universal assertion or factual claim.

Even here, however, Kierkegaard has reservations. There is the general point that not all truths are of this kind. Of some truths, he writes,

The knowledge in question does not lend itself to direct utter-
ance, because its essential feature consists of the appropriation.[38]

Within this category fall certain truths about self, truths that is to
say, of self-knowledge, and to these we shall turn in a moment.

There is, however, the more specific point that many truths of
which we believe ourselves to have certain knowledge, truths
which we communicate directly, are not quite as certain as they
seem. Recognition of this fact, a perennial stimulus to philosophers
from the pre-Socratics through Descartes and Hume to the present
day, lay at the root of Kierkegaard's praise both for Socratic
ignorance, and for philosophical scepticism. Neither Socrates, nor
the sceptics suffered from the illusion that some form of absolute
certainty can be gained through objective truths:

> Negative thinkers therefore always have one advantage, in that
> they have something positive, being aware of the negative ele-
> ment, in existence; the positive have nothing at all, since they
> are deceived.[39]

Kierkegaard did not, however, wish to advocate scepticism as a
final philosophical resting-place, but he did underline the value of
questioning the certainty of the objective truths of history. Whereas
radical scepticism could result in complete relativism Kierkegaard
wished rather to emphasize the more limited conclusion that history does not yield absolute of 'infinite' certainty: at most it offers
us 'approximate-knowledge'.

In dealing with this point Kierkegaard both offers and then
qualifies what seems to be a Cartesian solution to the dilemma:

> Nothing historical can become infinitely certain for me except
> the fact of my own existence ... and this is not something
> historical.[40]

There is, of course something paradoxical in such a qualification
for, of course, in one sense at least, our existence is historical. As
we have already noted it is of the essence of the human condition
that we are temporal beings. Kierkegaard's response, however, is

that although temporality is one of the conditions of human life, it is insufficient as an ideal defining characteristic:

> To have been young, and then to grow older, and finally to die is a very mediocre form of human existence: this merit belongs to any animal.[41]

The other sense of human existence, however, is, as we have seen, quite fundamental to Kierkegaard's writings.

> The real subject is the ethically existing subject.[42]

The genuine human being is only adequately characterized,

> as a synthesis of the finite and the infinite, (who) finds his reality in holding these two factors together, infinitely interested in existing.[43]

For Kierkegaard, the ethical is to be equated with 'infinite interest in one's own existence'. This is not, however, a crude form of ethical egoism, although it could certainly easily become a sophisticated embodiment of that doctrine. It is, I suggest, a version of the Socratic link between goodness, integrity, and self-knowledge. The ethical, on this view, is characterized by the search for self-knowledge. The ethical, however, is not simply a search for knowledge of what one is, or happens to be, it is a search for one's *telos*, a search for what one is potentially, for what is final, ultimate, eternal.

This, however, generates difficulties. The ethical demands that I know my potential, what is finally, ultimately or eternally true of myself. Yet one is finite: one is continually in a state of becoming, of process. There *is* no final state to be determined within or without oneself. One can certainly know oneself as finite, as becoming, as temporal, and it is essential that we should. But that in itself is not the final or ultimate truth about me. What it omits is precisely what differentiates me from an animal. It omits that I know myself, and that I can reflect on myself in this way. Even more important, it omits the recognition of the 'indefeasible claim' of the ethical, which I do recognize and which I do accept, that I should seek to know myself and my *telos*.

The argument then is this. Our existence is not swallowed up by our temporality, and self-knowledge is on that count, not knowledge of what is temporally true of us. Self-knowledge includes knowledge of what is a-historical. As temporal beings we cannot have such knowledge. There are two ways in which the argument can proceed. One, which Kierkegaard rejects, is towards scepticism as the last or final word. The other is to seek for some a-temporal truth about ourselves which once grasped will provide us with the elusive self-knowledge. One obvious possibility is that explored by Kant and the possibility of knowledge of ourselves as ethical beings seems indeed to be endorsed by Kierkegaard as the goal of our search.

The ethical is the search for one's *telos* and this necessity of such an interrogation of one's being is part of the 'indefeasible claim' of the ethical noted earlier. Yet, insofar as it *is* a search for one's *telos* it cannot produce the infinite certainty of knowledge. One is always *qua* temporal, in a state of becoming. There is no final resting-place, no characterization of the good for man, man's *telos*, which can be directly communicated. My *telos*, my ultimate happiness, lies through self-knowledge of my potentiality, but since I am continually in a state of becoming, this 'indefeasible claim', which I accept and in so doing, impose upon myself, *cannot* be met.

This has the form of a Kantian antinomy. What ethics demands, I cannot fulfil, but not, as in Kant, because contingencies separate the two elements of the highest good (virtue, and happiness in proportion to virtue), but because my essential state, one of becoming, makes such 'final' knowledge objectively impossible. Kant's way out of this particular difficulty was the postulation of God as the ground of the reconciliation of the two.[44] Kierkegaard could not accept such a move and made two alternative, cognate suggestions. On the one hand he was prepared to accept, and at times apparently almost to rejoice in, situations where one is faced with two *prima-facie* irreconcilable claims. He was thus prepared in a way certainly not true of Kant, to affirm that the irreconcilables constituted what must be seen objectively speaking, as a paradox.

This is, of course, a dangerous path to tread, and invites a specific version of the general question set by Ronald Hepburn:

> When is a contradiction not a *mere* contradiction, but a sublime Paradox, a Mystery?[45]

The penetration of this question loses none of its force when applied to Kierkegaard, and it is not clear to me that an incontestable reply can be given. Two points can, however, be adduced to obviate the charge of incoherence. One by implication has already been cited: not all truths are objective. The second is implicit in Kierkegaard's second alternative suggestion to a Kantian type of resolution of the difficulty. I refer here to Kierkegaard's stress on how one *appropriates* such self-knowledge. What this amounts to by way of response to Hepburn's question, is as follows. The self-knowledge demanded of men, yet denied them, is the self-knowledge objectively stated in these contradictory terms. This is the only possible form which such direct communication may take. The possibility of giving indirect communication to this truth, is conditional upon there being a pattern of life which is expressive of acceptance of both of the apparent irreconcilables. Kierkegaard believed that such a pattern could not have an ultimately distinctive outward form: such distinctiveness as there is, would be inner. Roy Holland makes the point in this way:

> ... the first precept for one who would attain to inwardness is γνῶθι σεαυτόν .... But awareness of what one is (of one's motives as they are) would be impossible without a conception of what one might have been or might become (a conception of one's motives as they ought to be – the conception of the ethical reality in accordance with which the maker of an external resolution strives and wills). Accordingly the search, insofar as it establishes anything, is said by Kierkegaard to establish that one is guilty and a sinner; and this result was foreshadowed from the start. As to the validity of the result, one's guarantee is the quality of the search. The quality of one's relationship to a τέλος is the guarantee of the absoluteness of that τέλος. It is one's relationship to eternity that defines it as eternity.[46]

In the nature of the case, then Kierkegaard can offer no objective answer to Hepburn's question. The implication of the points made above, is that what one makes of this, will depend in part, upon how one views the pattern of life which is offered by Kierkegaard as the only possible 'guarantee', or definition', (Holland's words) of the absoluteness of the τέλος.

A shift has been taking place in the discussion, and we now find ourselves confronting the question of the manner of life which is 'genuine ethical existence'. It is, as we have seen, a life that is inner in its directedness. It is a life in search of self-knowledge, a life focussed upon the eternal. What manner of life is that? Kierkegaard warns us that it is not a life which can be sketched in the detail of actuality. It may only be represented as a possibility:

> ... existential reality is incommunicable, and the subjective thinker finds his reality in his own ethical existence ...
> ... Whatever is great in the sphere of the universally human must therefore not be communicated as a subject for admiration but as an ethical requirement. In the form of a possibility it becomes a requirement. Instead of presenting an account of the good in the form of actuality, as is usually done, instead of insisting that such and such a person has actually lived, and has really done this or that, by which the reader is transformed into an admiring spectator, a critical connoisseur, the good should be presented in the form of a possibility.[47]

The presentation of goodness in the form of actuality is dangerous in three ways. First it may result in admiration rather than a sense of ethical requirement: a great man, a hero, is after all rather set apart from the common run of men. Perhaps this applies too, to his ethical 'achievement'. Second, if one attempts to portray goodness in this way, one is trying to communicate directly what is uncommunicable, namely, ethical, existence which is grasped only in the process of appropriation, not in the process or form of direct communication. Third, it could seem as if goodness has a particular contingent form which can be represented in this way.

For Kierkegaard 'only in the ethical is there to be found immortality and eternal life',[48] and we might legitimately reverse this to insist that 'only in the eternal is there to be found ethical life or existence'. The representation or (direct) communication of the eternal is, as we have seen, impossible. The same is true of the ethical, of goodness. In his meditation, *Purity of Heart is to Will One Thing*[49] Kierkegaard steadfastly refuses to say anything positive about goodness and purity other than that it is a unity, 'one thing'. Readers who search for a concise summary of what this 'one thing' is, search in vain. Students looking for Kierkegaard's definition of 'the Good' find only frustration. One is almost tempted to say 'there is no one thing which is for Kierkegaard, the Good', and in a sense this is true. No one actuality of contingent deeds and decisions is, or ever could be 'the Good'.

> To will only one thing: but will this not inevitably become a long-drawn-out talk? If one should consider this matter properly must he not first consider, one by one each goal in life that a man could conceivably set up for himself, mentioning separately all of the many things that a man might will?[50]

Would not this be an appropriate way of proceeding, to consider whether happiness, wisdom, pleasure, success, power, or contemplation, is *the* Good?

This will not do, for it leads to a separation of means and end. The goal is set, and the means are then devised of best achieving it.

> Eternally speaking, there is only one means and there is only one end: the means and the end are one and the same thing. There is only one end: the genuine Good; and the only one means; this, to be willing to use those means which genuinely are good – but the genuine Good is precisely the end.[51]

The separation of means and end in this context is unsatisfactory for a number of reasons. On the one hand, one can always ask of *any* particular end, is it good? i.e. the specification of some particular end as the Good, is always contentious. It does not carry the mark of its own authenticity on it. Kierkegaard makes this point in his own way when he stresses the importance of 'eternity's accounting', which asks only about 'the ultimate thing'. Such a question about any goal specified other than as 'the Good' is always, 'eternally', possible.

A second reason for dissatisfaction with the separation of means and end in this way, relates to what Kierkegaard means when he talks of 'eternity' and 'immortality'. He talks of 'eternity's accounting' where the only voice heard is that of conscience, but in so doing he is not talking about some future event. This distinguishes his talk of immortality and its significance for ethics very severely from that of say, Kant, for whom as for many Christian thinkers immortality means some form of post-mortem existence. For Kierkegaard,

> Immortality cannot be a final alteration that crept in, so to speak, at the moment of death as the final stage. On the contrary it is a changelessness that is not altered by the passage of the years.

He adds,

> If there is then, something eternal in a man, it must be able to exist and to be grasped within every change.[52]

To set oneself a goal, and to deliberate upon the means to achieve it may be both wise and prudent, but it is not the mark of the eternal in one's life, nor is it to be confused with purity of heart.

To set oneself a goal, however admirable, be it wisdom or happiness, is to define what is to be achieved and that in itself rules it out as 'the eternal', for two reasons. The first is the delusion that the eternal in life can be either defined or objectively communicated. Second, it makes purity and goodness depend upon the way things go: if one achieves one's goal then one has become pure: if not, for *any* reason, then one has failed. Kierkegaard would not deny the possibility of failure, but not because 'things did not quite go as expected'. If there is something eternal in a man, 'it must be able to exist and be grasped within *every* change'. No down-turn in one's fortunes should inevitably separate a man from eternity. Yet if he is simply at the stage of employing *means* towards an end, education towards wisdom, then some affliction, or death itself, may come between a man and *that* goal. Only something changeless in man can be the mark of the eternal. And the only thing that could possibly be changeless in man is the purity of heart which provides the perspective of eternity on his doing and his deciding:

> This consciousness (of considering one's life before God) is the fundamental condition for truthfully willing only one thing. For he who is not himself a unity is never really anything wholly and decisively.

> For after all, what is eternity's accounting other than that the voice of conscience is forever installed with its eternal right to be the exclusive voice.[53]

No one pattern, no one goal, can be separately identified as 'the Good', and the one thing which we must will if we seek purity of heart is not, either riches or poverty, either wisdom or foolishness, either talents or mediocrity, either celibacy or marriage. The one thing which we must will is the perspective of eternity on these and, of course, the perspective of eternity is not a vantage-point (goal) to be achieved, it is a manner of living realized only in the appropriation of it.

I want to conclude my comments on this topic with two further points. Kierkegaard leaves us no secure means of ensuring that our vantage point is that of eternity. This is part of the suffering of the individual, as well as his ethical fate. If one is ultimately and totally responsible in one's inwardness, for what one is, and what one does, there are no excuses, and no safeguards. This, of course, constitutes the frightening danger in such an idea, a danger which extends to those with whom one lives. A second point arises from Kierkegaard's later journals. There Kierkegaard shows himself well aware of the havoc which a rogue may attempt to create by appeal to a strongly Lutheran sense of inwardness.

> One treats a rascal, quite simply, by asking him, 'May I see your works?' If he comes along and assures you that he is ready to sacrifice everything in hidden inwardness, that in hidden inwardness he longs to sit and sing hymns and to fast in the silence of a monastery, while in his outward and visible life he is after profits and is a gallant in society, then you say to him – and this

is the simplicity in the matter – 'No, my dear friend, you must excuse me ... we want to see your works. Alas, how very necessary that is for us men!'[54]

Kierkegaard had no illusions about the capacity which most men had to self-deception, nor of how far the notions of inwardness and justification by faith lend themselves superficially to exploitation.

V

In conclusion it would be valuable to retrace our steps to the starting point of Kierkegaard as belonging to the discussions of the borderlands. In this he is at one with Hume. Also in unison, he calls for a new map of these self-same borderlands and of the difference between belief and unbelief which must first be drawn accurately from this perspective. As Hume tried to do this by inhabiting both sides of the border in the characters of his *Dialogues*, so too Kierkegaard used dialogue form: on the one hand most obviously within particular works; but on the other, more tellingly *between* different works – the aesthetic and the religious. Even more significantly, as we noticed, Kierkegaard adopts in places the standpoint of 'an outsider' to faith whose sole qualification for the role given to him is that he can see clearly what the differences are between belief and unbelief.

Kierkegaard's belief in the need to write under such a pseudonym has complex roots but one element is certainly the unclarity and ambiguity which he found in his own day over what it was to be a Christian. The consequence of this is that at best there will be those who are trying to become Christians, to discover what if anything that might mean.

How far Christianity is from existing can best be seen from my own case.

For with such clarity as I have I must say that I am not a Christian. For the situation as I see it is that in spite of the abyss of nonsense in which we are caught, we shall all alike be saved.

This is the consequence of having as a child acquired a so-called Christianity which is just the reverse.

But my position is certainly difficult enough. I am not like a pagan, to whom an apostle briefly and emphatically proclaims Christianity; no, I am the one who, so to say, himself must discover it, work it out, from the perverted state to which it has been reduced.[55]

The map of the borderlands has been redrawn and in such a way as to put the question of what it is to be a Christian on a very different plain from that sketched by Hume. But the central residual question remains of whether a coherent intelligible account of what it is to be a Christian can be given.

Kierkegaard shares with Hume a rejection of the arguments of traditional natural theology, for both insist upon the invalidity of arguments from the natural world to the existence of a transcendent God. Kierkegaard agrees with Hume further, that in at least one sense the dispute about such a God is 'mere verbal controversy'. The difference however, is that Kierkegaard's point is that *direct* communication about God is impossible: but this allows the possibility of *indirect* communication.

Thus in one sense even for Kierkegaard ambiguity is of the essence of faith, for one can only communicate indirectly and to that extent ambiguously. The ambiguity is of a very different form from that found in either Dostoyevsky or Hume, but its importance cannot be denied.

4

SIMONE WEIL AND
ALBERT CAMUS

The ambiguity of the borderlands situation receives its definitive twentieth-century exemplification in the relationship between Albert Camus and Simone Weil. The extent of the ties between them has been discussed surprisingly little, and one of the earliest references to this, in 1960, by Czeslaw Milozy refers appropriately to the 'hidden ties' between Simone Weil and Albert Camus.[1]

Albert Camus speaks the language of Rebellion. His novel *The Outsider*, pre-dated the 'beat-generation' of Kerouac by a decade and a half, and the student-revolt of the sixties by a quarter of a century. The serrated edge of Meursault's tongue still leaves scars on the established religion of the prison chaplain, and simultaneously disengages his spirit from the artificial virtues of church and society:

> For quite a while he kept his eyes averted. His presence was getting more and more irksome, and I was on the point of telling him to go, and leave me in peace, when all of a sudden he swung round on me, and burst out passionately:
> 'No! No! I refuse to believe it. I'm sure you've often wished there was an after-life.'
> Of course I had, I told him. Everybody has that wish at times. But that had no more importance than wishing to be rich, or to swim very fast, or to have a better-shaped mouth. It was in the same order of things. I was going on in the same

vein, when he cut in with a question. How did I picture my life after the grave?

I fairly bawled out at him: 'A life in which I can remember this life on earth. That's all I want of it.' And in the same breath I told him I'd had enough of his company.

But, apparently, he had more to say on the subject of God. I went close up to him and made a last attempt to explain that I'd very little time left, and I wasn't going to waste it on God.

Then he tried to change the subject by asking me why I hadn't once addressed him as 'Father', seeing that he was a priest. That irritated me still more, and I told him he wasn't my father; quite the contrary, he was on the others' side.

'No, no, my son,' he said, laying his hand on my shoulder. 'I'm on *your* side, though you don't realise it – because your heart is hardened. But I shall pray for you.'

Then, I don't know how it was, but something seemed to break inside me, and I started yelling at the top of my voice. I hurled insults at him, I told him not to waste his rotten prayers on me; it was better to burn than to disappear. I'd taken him by the neckband of his cassock, and, in a sort of ecstasy of joy and rage, I poured out on him all the thoughts that had been simmering in my brain. He seemed so cocksure, you see. And yet none of his certainties was worth one strand of a woman's hair. Living as he did, like a corpse, he couldn't even be sure of being alive. It might look as if my hands were empty. Actually, I was sure of myself, sure about everything, far surer than he; sure of my present life and of the death that was coming. That, no doubt, was all I had; but at least that certainty was something I could get my teeth into – just as it had got its teeth into me. I'd been right, I was still right, I was always right. I'd pass my life in a certain way, and I might have passed it in a different way, if I'd felt like it. I'd acted thus, and I hadn't acted otherwise; I hadn't done *x*, whereas I had done *y* or *z*. And what did that mean? That all the time, I'd been waiting for this present moment, for that dawn, tomorrow's or another day's, which was to justify me. Nothing, nothing had the least importance, and I knew quite well why. He, too, knew why. From the dark horizon of my future a sort of slow, persistent breeze had been blowing towards me, all my life long, from the years that were to come. And on its way that breeze had levelled out all the ideas that people tried to foist on me in the equally unreal years I then was living through. What a difference could they make to me, the death of others, or a mother's love, or his God; or the way one decides to live, the fate one thinks one chooses, since one and the same fate was bound to 'choose' not only me but thousands of millions of privileged people who, like him, called themselves my brothers. Surely, surely he must see that? Every man alive was privileged; there was only one class of men, the privileged class. All alike would be condemned to die one day; his turn, too, would come like the others.[2]

Even in the tight, clipped suspicious times of economic retrenchment Meursault can briefly re-kindle the soused embers of rebellion in the human spirit. How else can we account for the remarkable sales and reprint record of the novel?

Meursault's rebellion was a rebellion of body and spirit. In his most important philosophical work *The Rebel* published in 1951, Camus demonstrated the organic link between body, spirit and mind in these matters and in so doing gave intellectual form and foundation to those inner stirrings of resistance and self-assertion which are part of the legacy of European history.

The present interest in the problem of rebellion only springs from the fact that nowadays whole societies have wanted to discard the sacred. We live in an unsacrosant moment in history.

The Metaphysical rebel declares that he is frustrated by the universe.[3]

Anger, passion, resentment, frustration – all key words in the vocabulary of Rebellion. How different, we might say, the spirit of Simone Weil:

To be what the pencil is for me when, blindfold, I feel the table by means of its point – to be that for Christ.

Obedience is the supreme virtue.

When I am in any place, I disturb the silence of heaven and earth by my breathing and the beating of my heart.[4]

To become something divine, I have no need to get away from my misery, I have only to adhere to it. My very sins are a help to me, on condition that I know how to read in them the full extent of my misery. It is in the deepest depth of my misery that I touch God.[5]

The accent, the tone of voice, and all that is carried in it, seems as far in spirit from Camus, as Nietzsche is from St Francis, or Father Zossima from Ivan Karamazov.

Is it then that we find unlikely ground for comparison between Simone Weil and Albert Camus? That is an understatement, for it would seem as if there is no common ground at all – as if there were an abyss separating belief from unbelief – Simone Weil from Albert Camus. Consider for example, what they say about suffering: Camus writes approvingly

Ivan (Karamazov) rejects the profound relationship, introduced by Christianity, between suffering and truth.[6]

Whereas Simone Weil, careful for the suffering of others, affirms nonetheless what Ivan and Camus reject:

One should not speak to those in affliction about the Kingdom of God, it is too remote from them, but only about the Cross. God suffered. Therefore suffering is a divine thing. In itself. Not because of compensations, consolations, recompenses. But the very suffering which inspires horror, which we endure against our will, which we seek to escape, which we beg to be spared. Affliction.[7]

Undoubtedly great issues are at stake in the differences which we see between Simone Weil and Albert Camus. I am equally certain however, that the impressionistic picture which has so far been created is quite distorted. There are two reasons for such distortion. The first is the eagerness which we all feel in our search for stereotypes, the delight with which we consign others to pigeon-holes ready warm and receptive to their intellectual captives. Our age may believe itself to be above the use of the terms 'heresy' and 'orthodoxy', but we have found alternative straight-jackets to confine the movement of the human spirit. 'Belief' and 'unbelief' – to these terms we have given in our perverse way, vague but constricting meanings – meanings which set the two far apart from each other, and each of which demands its pound of flesh. Woe betide the man or woman for whom the idea of truth takes priority. Thus we insist upon setting Camus and Simone Weil against one another – unlikely ground for comparison, but good fodder for opposing apologetic cannons. A ravine has been opened up between them, and a great deal has been lost, including the truth of the matter.

Camus is readily and wholly identified with the Meursault who in the condemned cell refused the consolations of religion, and companionship of the prison chaplain, and who found brotherhood only in 'the benign indifference of the universe'. There is a consequent temptation to see the confrontation between the theism of Paneloux and the humanism of Rieux which occasionally breaks through the surface of *The Plague* as a tract in antitheistic apologetics, and this does less than justice to the humanity and sensitivity of the author. The evidently agnostic or even atheistic views of Camus are annexed but annexed too easily. They are detached from the travail of intellect and spirit which gave them birth: they are often detached too from the humility and humanity in which they were nurtured – the humanity and humility which gave to Paneloux, who told his congregation,

> This same pestilence which is slaying you works for your good and points your path[8]

a, perhaps pathetic, nobility in death, but a nobility and serenity which none the less refuse to caricature his religious faith. A superficial and popular view of Camus focusses more easily upon those features of his thought which almost stridently seem to imply the worthlessness of religion, and Camus is enlisted upon the side of unbelief.

Conversely, such popular assessment of, and acquaintance with, Simone Weil that there has been, has placed her at the opposite end of the apologetic spectrum. She is gradually being assimilated into the respectable company of the faithful. Stress is laid upon her asceticism and mystical tendencies. More attention is paid to her later work, than to her earlier (pre-1938) writings; her very radical unorthodoxy tends to be ignored rather than examined.

The second reason for the distorted picture which, to mix metaphors, simply assigns Simone Weil and Albert Camus to different frames, is in fact ignorance. We have ignored what Camus has told us implicitly in his public writings and explicitly in his notebooks. To free ourselves from this particular form of intellectual bondage we turn initially and most obviously to Camus' own comment on Simone Weil.

It is most probable that Camus first became acquainted with Simone Weil's work towards the end of 1945, or at the beginning of 1946. His respect for her thought was such that he played an important part in arranging the posthumous publication of her writings. This was no mere liberal gesture towards respect for alternative views simply because they were alternative views: a few years later in an unsigned comment on Simone Weil's *The Need for Roots*[9] he writes of the work as,

> ... one of the most lucid, the most exalted, the most beautiful books on our civilization which has been written for a very long time ... This austere book with a forthrightness that is occasionally severe, unbending but at the same time admirably balanced, with a Christianity that is authentic and very pure, offers a lesson that is often bitter, but of an unusual elevation of thought.[10]

Undoubtedly Camus found much to respect and admire in Simone Weil – the later as well as the earlier work. In 1951 he described her as 'the only great spirit of our time'[11] and in *his* memoir Jean Grenier refers to two keys to Camus's work, 'the myth of Moby Dick and the thought of Simone Weil'.[12] Grenier agrees that this claim requires an amplification which he does not there offer, beyond quoting some of Camus's own words on the subject, and suggesting,

> The admiration he had for Melville and Simone Weil developed the sense of the mysterious and of the sacred, a sense which did not imply abandoning the sense of rebellion.

The implications, however, are sufficient to counterbalance any tendency to over-readily and superficially set Camus and Simone Weil apart. Also it points one to parts of Camus's own work which can be easily neglected, or undervalued.

A distinguishing feature of Camus's humanism is its humility, intellectual, moral, and spiritual. One way of viewing a central theme of his work is as an attempt to define a form of humanism which preserves this humility, a humanism which gives man hope without accompanying delusions of immortality or aspirations towards 'superhumanity'. The dangers he saw here are moral and spiritual and as he saw around him, perhaps most pointedly during the Nazi occupation of France, such loss of humility in one's humanism, such belief in the potential 'superhumanity' of men can lead to political totalitarianism, just as easily as did a belief in superior religious insight in previous centuries. One of the pivots of his development is the move in *The Plague* from what he calls 'le point zero' of *The Outsider* and *The Myth of Sisyphus* not towards the infinite, but towards 'a deeper complexity which has still to be defined'.[13] It is this deeper complexity which much of Camus's subsequent work sought to define. The levels at which this definition was to be formulated were twofold: at a conceptual or philosophical level Camus was struggling to find categories in which to delineate and preserve a humanism which did not seek superhumanism; at a level which may be distinguished from this analytically, although not in Camus's life and writings, he was attempting to delineate a form or style of life appropriate to this century. To be articulate about the latter is, in fact, to have succeeded in the former.

Part of the fruits of this search is his use of the notion of 'limits' in the concluding sections of *The Rebel*. By then the notion was radically secular, and as early as 1945–6, we find Camus attempting to specify precisely what he means by this term:

> Limits. By this I mean that there are mysteries which one must enumerate and consider. Nothing more.[14]

Much earlier in the notebooks, however, despite a sarcastic outburst against those critics of *The Outsider* who confuse manliness with prophetic flutterings, and greatness with spiritual affection, one terse remark does suggest that he had not initially completely ruled out the use of religious categories to delineate his task:

> Secret of my world: To imagine God without human immortality.[15]

My suggestion here is that Camus's primary concern is to define a particular form of humanism rather than to reject theism as such. In the interests of a clear statement of what this humanism amounts to he would have been quite willing to use the language and thought forms of religion – 'to imagine God without human immortality'. In fact, he did come to reject these thought forms as inimical to his enterprise, for those concepts of religion, those parts of the language of religion which, if salvageable, might have helped him in his task, he came to see as too bound up with those aspects of Christian belief, which were incompatible with the position which he was formulating. For example, he came to see as an integral part of the Christian religion the doctrine of original sin, and what he refers to in *The Rebel* as 'the profound relationship, introduced by Christianity, between suffering and truth'[16]: neither of these, he believed, was compatible with the stance of rebellion.

Although he came to reject the concept of God as anything more than a focus of certain sorts of rebellion, he did not, for example, reject the notions of 'the sacred' and 'the mysterious', basically religious notions. Indeed they were important to his enterprise: important in that they helped delineate the notion of 'limits' which is crucial for his hope of defining the progress towards 'a deeper complexity' whose direction was laid down in *The Plague*. There was and continued to be for Camus an interest in the possibilities offered by the language and thought of religion.

Much of the language of religion he rejected because he did not see any way of detaching it in satisfactory manner from those aspects of religion which he rejected utterly. His respect for Simone Weil must, in part, have been a respect for someone who found the language and thought-forms of religion more pliable, more fertile. In some way, parts of what can be called her 'humanism' must have been highly congenial to his own estimate of the men of his age. He must have had more than a passing interest in the work of a kindred spirit, not least when that kindred spirit was prepared to be much more bold, or less damning, depending upon one's point of view, in her retention of the language and thought-forms of religion.

The notion of a 'kindred spirit', however, directs us to two further points of convergence between these two thinkers. Initially and basically as has already been implied in what has gone before, both were in search of what we might call a *form* or *style* of life appropriate to their age. Nothing less than this, be it intellectual insight, literary success, religious or aesthetic experience, would satisfy. Indeed it was this aspect of Christianity alone which won Camus's respect and possibly even admiration:

> What is it that constitutes the pre-eminence of the example (but of that alone) of Christianity? Christ and his saints – the quest for a *style of life*.[17]

Simone Weil clearly is in step with *that* aspect of Christianity: for her the total direction of thought, word, and deed, was towards defining and achieving that integrity which is complete unity and coherence in life. And integrity is, indeed, the second point of convergence between these kindred spirits. Camus's respect for *The Need for Roots* would by no means be diminished by the following sentences:

> . . . for religious feeling to emanate from the spirit of truth, one should be absolutely prepared to abandon one's religion, even if that should mean losing all motive for living, if it should turn out to be anything other than the truth. In this state of mind alone it is possible to discern whether there is truth in it. Other-

wise one doesn't venture even to propound the problem in all
its rigour.[18]

A point of common intellectual outlook which derived from these
similarities of inclination and personality, is distate for abstractions
in thought. In fact Roy Pierce identifies this as 'the main link'
between the thought of Camus and Simone Weil. This is to place
perhaps too much emphasis on a point which both must have
shared with many of their contemporaries, for example, aspects
of Sartre's thought in France, and of Wittgenstein's in Britain
during the 1930s and 40s. It is nonetheless there, whether implicitly in Camus's detailed descriptions of character, climate and
situation in the novels, or explicitly in Simone Weil's plea for
precision in the meaning, use, and analysis of words in her 1937
paper 'The Power of Words'.[19]

More crucial and already foreshadowed is the extent to which
each, in search of an adequate life-style, was what one can only
call 'anti-positivist'. Amongst the myths of the age to be rejected
must be included the positivist myth of progress, based on science
alone, the approach to social and political questions which
Dostoyevsky pilloried under the label 'calculemus', and one of
whose leading exponents he identified as Claude Bernard. It was
in the face of this illusion that Camus developed his notion of
'limits', here that even he felt the need to preserve the language,
and thus consciousness, of 'mystery'. Simone Weil's deep knowledge of the history of science is the foundation of her many
writings on scientific topics and is one of the two pillars of her
scorn for 'scientism', whether stemming from the physical, social,
or biological sciences. The other pillar, 'the need for roots', and
the understanding of the spiritual and cultural roots of individuals
and people as a prerequisite for a proper appreciation of who and
what they are, comes out in her witty comment on the 1937
Exhibition in Paris:

The 1937 Exhibition, already so far from us, was to some extent
a manifestation of contemporary scientism; an extremely
cultured man, high in the university hierarchy, seriously wished

after visiting it that in every village in France the church might be replaced by a miniature Palace of Discovery.[20]

That Camus was impressed by what Simone Weil said on the subject is clear from the fact that he quotes the following remark from *The Need for Roots* in his notebooks:

> If justice is ineradicable from the spirit of man, then it has a reality in this world. It is science therefore which is wrong.

Then he comments:

> S.W. Contradiction between science and humanism. No. Between the scientific outlook called modern, and humanism. For it is determinism and power which disowns man.[21]

It is difficult to decide on the basis of this entry alone whether Camus intends the 'No' to be attributed to Simone Weil or to himself. However, from the appropriate section of *The Need for Roots*, it is quite clear that the 'No' belongs to Simone Weil, and Camus who, from the entries in *The Notebooks* seems to have been reading the text of *The Need for Roots* at this time (April–June 1948), prior to its publication 1949, would have been well aware that there was no need to correct Simone Weil on this point: she of all his contemporaries was well aware of the possibility of an alternative view of science, e.g., that of the Greeks.

In the light of this view of Camus, I find puzzling Grenier's remark that Camus is in agreement with Simone Weil, in *The Plague* – 'where science and religion are portrayed as antagonists'.[22] Grenier supports this with a quotation from *The Need for Roots* in which Simone Weil speaks of the absolute incompatibility which Christians find between religion and science, but as the context makes clear, it is an incompatibility between religion, and the science called 'modern' to which she points. Conversely, when in *The Plague* there is an antagonism between Father Paneloux and Dr Rieux, the antagonism has little to do with positivistic objections to religion: it is more a matter of the disjunction between on the one hand Camus's version of humanism, which cannot interpret the death of small children as 'working for your good', or 'pointing your path', and on the other hand the theology of Father Paneloux's first sermon. As such, as we shall see, it is not far from Simone Weil, but is not essentially a matter of the contrast between religion and science. A more interesting point of convergence in relation to *The Plague*, arises from Simone Weil's unwitting use of the situation of *The Plague* as an analogy for the need for saints. Talking of the demand of the present moment for a new form of saintliness, one based in genius rather than intellectual gifts, she continues,

> The world needs saints who have genius, just as a plague-stricken town needs doctors. Where there is a need there is also an obligation.[23]

Elsewhere she tells us that by 'genius' she means something quite different from 'intellectually gifted'.

> Genius is – perhaps – nothing other than the ability to go through 'dark nights'.[24]

In this context her use of the image of a plague-stricken town, the connection implied between need and obligation, cannot fail to call to mind Tarrou's probing questions to Dr Rieux.

> 'My question's this,' said Tarrou. 'Why do you yourself show such devotion, considering you don't believe in God? I suspect your answer may help me to mine.'
>
> His face still in shadow, Rieux said that he'd already answered: that if he believed in an all-powerful God he would cease curing the sick and leave that to Him. But no one in the world believed in a God of that sort; not even Paneloux, who believed that he believed in such a God. And this was proved by the fact that no one ever threw himself on Providence completely. Anyhow, in this respect Rieux believed himself to be on the right road – in fighting against creation as he found it.
>
> 'Ah', Tarrou remarked. 'So that's the idea you have of your profession?'
>
> 'More or less.' The doctor came back into the light.
>
> Tarrou made a faint whistling noise with his lips, and the doctor gazed at him.

'Yes, you're thinking it calls for pride to feel that way. But I assure you I've no more than the pride that's needed to keep me going. I have no idea what's awaiting me, or what will happen when all this ends. For the moment I know this; there are sick people and they need curing. Later on, perhaps, they'll think things over; and so shall I. But what's wanted now is to make them well. I defend them as best I can, that's all.'

'Against whom?'

Rieux turned to the window. A shadow-line on the horizon told of the presence of the sea. He was conscious only of his exhaustion, and at the same time was struggling against a sudden, irrational impulse to unburden himself a little more to his companion; an eccentric, perhaps, but who, he guessed, was one of his own kind.

'I haven't a notion, Tarrou; I assure you I haven't a notion. When I entered this profession, I did it "abstractedly", so to speak; because I had a desire for it, because it meant a career like another, one that young men often aspire to. Perhaps, too, because it was particularly difficult for a workman's son, like myself . . . And then I had to see people die. Do you know that there are some who *refuse* to die? Have you ever heard a woman scream "Never!" with her last gasp? Well, I have. And then I saw that I could never get hardened to it. I was young then, and I was outraged by the whole scheme of things, or so I thought. Subsequently, I grew more modest. Only, I've never managed to get used to seeing people die. That's all I know. Yet after all . . .'

Rieux fell silent, and sat down. He felt his mouth dry.

'After all . . .?' Tarrou prompted softly.

'After all,' the doctor repeated, then hesitated again, fixing his eyes on Tarrou, 'it's something that a man of your sort can understand most likely, but, since the order of the world is shaped by death, mightn't it be better for God if we refuse to believe in Him, and struggle with all our might against death, without raising our eyes towards the heaven where He sits in silence?'

Tarrou nodded.

'Yes. But your victories will never be lasting; that's all.'

Rieux's face darkened.

'Yes, I know that. But it's no reason for giving up the struggle.'

'No reason, I agree . . . Only, I now can picture what this plague must mean for you.'

'Yes. A never-ending defeat.'

Tarrou stared at the doctor for a moment, then turned and tramped heavily towards the door. Rieux followed him and was almost at his side when Tarrou, who was staring at the floor suddenly said:

'Who taught you all this, doctor?'

The reply came promptly.

'Suffering.'[25]

Tarrou's response to the plague is the response of obligation defined by the needs of those who suffer and this of course is the precise exemplification of the general principle enunciated at the outset of *The Need for Roots*:

> . . . the list of obligations towards the human being should correspond to the list of such human needs as are vital analogous to hunger.[26]

The fact that additionally Simone Weil uses elsewhere the image of a plague-stricken town to illustrate her concept of saintliness is undoubtedly a coincidence – but coincidence of image can be a profoundly suggestive clue to coincidence of spirit. Perhaps the proximity between Simone Weil and Albert Camus, perhaps the admiration of the latter for the former lies in the fact that the pointer to Simone Weil's account of the style of life appropriate to Christianity in the twentieth century is to be found in Dr Rieux rather than in Father Paneloux. Both Simone Weil and Albert Camus, would, I suggest, find Paneloux's religion inadequate. In the 1940s at least, Camus offers us Rieux as the first step towards 'a deeper complexity which has yet to be defined'. In the 1940s also Simone Weil appeals, if only in passing, to the same parable of a town beleaguered by plague to give a secular outline or point of departure for her concept of saintliness. This consciousness of the obligations created by need is perhaps the deepest point of convergence between these two thinkers. The divergences begin to occur as each attempts to define the form of response appropriate to the needs of their age. In great measure they shared a conception, on at least one level, of what those needs were. But of course, the fact that two thinkers of rigour, coherence and integrity, in the end do propose different responses, does imply that at some deeper level yet to be uncovered, they *did* disagree in their diagnosis of the needs of their age.

Clearly, then, an over-ready disposition to set Simone Weil and Albert Camus apart as aggressive atheist and devoted defender of the faith is a sign of superficiality. Their common inheritance, the sympathy with which Camus received Simone Weil's diagnosis of the spiritual needs of the age would in themselves be sufficient to dispose of that untruth. On the other hand a concentration on the affinities and overlaps to be discovered in their writings could lead one to the converse error of assuming that in the end there is little significant difference to be found. In keeping with the mood of some contemporary churchmen in pursuit of 'reconciliation', it might be easy to begin to obscure the deep differences which do separate Simone Weil from Albert Camus. In a talk given at a Dominican Monastery in 1948, Camus protests at such intellectual facility:

> The other day at the Sorbonne, speaking to a Marxist lecturer, a Catholic priest said in public that he, too, was anti-clerical. Well, I don't like priests who are anti-clerical any more than philosophies that are ashamed of themselves. Hence I shall not try to pass myself off as a Christian in your presence. I share with you the same revulsion from evil. But I do not share your hope and I continue to struggle against this universe in which children suffer and die.

In the face of a world of suffering and death, Camus's response is one of struggle and rebellion: here the chasm between them opens, for Camus could not speak, as Simone Weil did, of the order of the world as the beauty of the world, and this because there is a deep sense in which he would view with abhorrence her assertion that

> the order of the world is to be loved because it is pure obedience to God.[27]

Any suggestion, however, that Simone Weil could only make such claims if she were insensitive to the suffering of others must be based on total ignorance of her life and her writings.

What alternative accounts may then be given of this radical disjunction in their respective responses to the world in which they live? One clue here is Grenier's remark that what alienated Camus from Simone Weil was his lack of affinity with people who did not 'enjoy being happy'. Another is the connection between this partial view of Simone Weil and the rather wistful and perhaps musing remark in *Carnets* II,

> For quite a time I have lived, lamenting, in the world of the flesh, but I have admired those who, like Simone Weil, seem to escape from there. For my part I could not imagine love without possession, and therefore without the humiliating agony which is the lot of those who love according to the flesh.[28]

The suggested conception of love here is basically one of possession and as we shall see, an understanding of what in the end does separate Simone Weil from Camus, will involve grasping the significance for her of a quite different conception of what love can be. To see the significance of all this we must return to the question of suffering within the world, and particularly the suffering of the innocent. It is the strength of Simone Weil's thought that she made response to suffering central to her understanding of Christianity. She, like Camus, started with a realistic assessment of the world in which she lived: it was a world in which the marks of pain and suffering lay all around. For Camus the failure of Christianity lay in the 'profound relationship' which it introduced 'between suffering and truth'. The fear which he shared with Ivan Karamazov is that such a faith 'presumes the acceptance of ... evil and resignation to injustice'. One version of what this can

amount to is to be found in Paneloux's first sermon, and that
Camus rightly rejects. But so also does Simone Weil. Fundamentally she insists that in some sense one must accept suffering in
the world, but she wants *also*,

> to say like Ivan Karamazov: nothing can possibly make up for
> a single tear from a single child.[29]

Her sympathies are, at this point, undoubtedly with Rieux and
Ivan rather than Paneloux. Suffering is not acceptable because it
might be compensated for, nor because it is the will of God. 'The
reverse way is purer. (Perhaps . . .)'. Again she tells Father Perrin
that the one thing which prevents certainty and which comes
between her and the love of God, is the affliction of others,
particularly those who are remote from her in time and relationship.

> There is only one time when I really know nothing of this
> certitude any longer. It is when I am in contact with the afflic-
> tion of other people, those who are indifferent or unknown to
> me as much as the others, perhaps even more, including those
> of the most remote ages of antiquity. This contact causes me
> such atrocious pain and so utterly rends my soul, that as a
> result the love of God becomes almost impossible for me for a
> while. It would take very little more to make me say impossible.
> So much so that I am uneasy about myself, I reassure myself a
> little by remembering that Christ wept on foreseeing the hor-
> rors of the destruction of Jerusalem. I hope he will forgive me
> my compassion.[30]

In the end, however, she explicitly and firmly rejects the position
of both Ivan and Camus. Her reasons for rejection are subtle but
the gap between revolt and rebellion on the one hand, and on the
other, her belief that affliction must not simply be accepted but
rather viewed as a gift, is wide as it is fundamental. There are three
different sorts of considerations which lead her away from rather
than towards rebellion. In the first case,

> to rebel against God because of man's affliction, after the manner

of Vigny or Ivan Karamazov, is to represent God to oneself as a sovereign.[31]

Such was not Simone Weil's conception of God, nor was this a view of God which she believed to be central to Christianity. It was rather a combination of the Old Testament conception of Jehovah, and the result of the establishment of Christianity as the state religion of the Roman Empire. Undoubtedly it had been influential within the history of the church, but it was an error, a deviation from the Christian conception of God, which, according to Simone Weil, is based in part at least on a kenotic christology. God is found and loved only as the God who has emptied himself of his divinity. God as sovereign on the other hand is a God who can evoke the response of fear or anger. Such a God is a natural God, against whom rebellion may be foolhardy, but it is at least intelligible: the God of the Christians is a supernatural God to whom the only adequate and appropriate relation is love. Here the negative points in her theology are much clearer than the positive claims, and to these latter we must return shortly. Initially, however, her protest at Ivan's rebellion is that it is revolt against an anthropomorphic or natural God.

Her second sort of objection seems to have a *prima facie* basis in an understanding of the psychology of rebellion and revolt. Her fear was that what begins as an act of compassion for the afflictions of others may end as an act of self-assertion. As such it would have left compassion behind. The significance of this argument, however, is not simply that of a belief about the contingent facts of human psychology. It has to do with what she saw as the conceptual connections between acceptance and compassion. What Simone Weil means by the 'acceptance' of affliction and suffering, whether in one's own case or in the case of others, is nothing more nor less than 'attention'. Attention which is complete and absolute is the form of love, whether the love of God or the love of one's neighbour. Attention as such is a form of self-emptying: it is contemplation of what is not-self; it is to be absorbed in what is other than oneself. As such, Simone Weil believed attention, and therefore love and compassion, to be incompatible with rebellion:

Those who rebel in the presence of affliction would like to *be* something.[32]

To want to be something is in the end the basic form of self-assertion. When self comes into the picture, one has to that extent diverted or averted one's eyes: one no longer attends to the affliction of others. This, I take it, is what Simone Weil means when she argues that rebellion consists in averting one's eyes, and that 'acceptance is nothing else than a quality of attention'. Camus would accept part at least of what is said here. Rebellion is in the first instances '*my own* protest'.[33] It is an act of self-assertion. Camus realized too that, as such, if guided only by historical expediency, it can become the self-assertion of tyranny. This is why at the end of *The Rebel*, he wants to insist that rebellion must be distinguished from resentment, and that it can be, but only in so far as one insists that 'rebellion cannot exist without a strange form of love'. What Simone Weil's account of the concepts of revolt, acceptance, attention and compassion implies, is that Camus's hope is a vain one: self-assertion cannot grow progressively into love that is selfless.

One possibility which she does allow, but the legitimacy of which she does not at that point fully grasp is put in the following way:

(If, in conclusion, he (Ivan Karamazov) were to say: 'I won't accept – not a single tear shall be shed over and above what it is strictly outside my power to prevent' – he would then possess the implicit love of God – but by what mechanism?)[34]

Despite the hesitant query of 'but by what mechanism?', what is being said here is compatible with the account given above of Simone Weil's thought. It is neither God nor his world which is not accepted here: what is not accepted is any response of one's own which is less than complete. What *is* accepted is the obligation created by the need of one's neighbour suffering affliction. This is not revolt or rebellion as the author of *The Rebel* and Ivan see revolt and rebellion. It is, however, the response of Rieux to Tarrou's insistent questioning:

Yes, you're thinking it calls for pride to feel that way. But I assure you I've no more than the pride that's needed to keep me going. I have no idea what's awaiting me, or what will happen when all this ends. For the moment I know this; they are sick people and they need curing. Later on, perhaps, they'll think things over; and so shall I. But what's wanted now is to make them well . . .

I was young then, and was outraged by the whole scheme of things, or so I thought. Subsequently, I grew more modest. Only I've never managed to get used to seeing people die. That's all I know . . .

. . . but, since the order of the world is shaped by death, mightn't it be better for God if we refuse to believe in Him, and struggle with all our might against death, without raising our eyes towards the heaven where He sits in silence?[35]

It is not the revolt which Rieux thought himself to have felt as a young man which leads him to respond as he does: it is the need of his patients, obligation defined by needs as Simone Weil defines obligation in *The Need for Roots*. It does too exemplify precisely what Simone Weill means when she talks of implicit love as absurd and supernatural, as the height of folly. Of course when Tarrou tells Rieux that his victories over death and suffering 'will never be lasting', Rieux can only reply 'But it's no reason for giving up the struggle'.

These kinds of love are supernatural, and in a sense they are absurd. They are the height of folly. So long as the soul has not had direct contact with the very person of God, they cannot be supported by any knowledge based either on experience or reason . . . In consequence it is better that they should not be associated with any belief. That is more honest intellectually and it safeguards our love's purity more effectively.[36]

This second sort of objection to rebellion and revolt, then, that if it remains rebellion, it rules out the love of compassion and self-giving, does not exclude the compassion of Rieux. What Rieux *does* refuse is 'to love a scheme of things in which children are put to torture'. Revolt, outraged rebellion against God, is for Rieux, however, in the end, 'mad revolt': even in giving way to it, he sees it as less than worthless, a positive distraction from the needs around him. It is, nonetheless a long step from this tangential point of agreement with Camus about the significance of a Rieux, to Simone Weil's insistence upon love of the order of the world, and, as we shall see, not one that she can make without, as she realizes, talking what is on one level, at least, nonsense.

The third sort of reason given in objection to the notions of rebellion and revolt, is the claim that the rebellion of Ivan is in the end a means of detaching himself from reality. We have already noted the central importance which Simone Weil attaches to a love of the order of the world. There is, however, a further connection which she makes between love and desire on the one hand, and acceptance on the other, the sense of which is on a first and indeed on a second hearing difficult to grasp. Consider the following sentences.

Not to accept some event taking place in the world is to desire that the world should not exist.[37]

To believe in the reality of the outside world and to love it – these are but one and the same thing.[38]

One must accept everything, all things, without any reservation, both inside and outside oneself, in the whole universe, with the same degree of love; but evil must be accepted as evil and good as good.[39]

Initially a point of clarification: it would of course be an elementary blunder to read these remarks as advocating quietism, whether moral or political. When she talks in the impersonal terms of an 'event' in the world, she is talking of those events over which we have no control, for example the tears and suffering which neither Ivan nor Rieux could prevent. Such events, she insists must be accepted in some sense Nor does she mean reluctantly or grudgingly accepted. They must in some sense be desired. Here desire is the opposite of protest or rebellion. Not to accept is not to desire; not to desire is to want things to be different. What, one may ask in the face of the crying child, is wrong with that? That of course, would be Rieux's question, and Camus's, and it illustrates the point at which despite his admiration for Simone Weil, Camus would part company from her. At one level the diversion is a division over what is to be made of suffering. As an interpreter of Christianity Camus often has greater insight than many of its adherents. He recognized and insisted upon,

> the profound relationship introduced by Christianity, between suffering and truth.

But in the end he rejected completely such a view of truth. Simone Weil accepted that suffering and truth are connected: in so doing she ruled out rebellion in the manner of Ivan, or of Camus. There *must* be some other way . . .

At a different level this shows in her rejection of the conception of God accepted, indeed *required*, by the rebel, but as we have already noticed, she was clearer here in what she rejected, than in that in her account of the alternative to atheism which is offered. Perhaps the most sustained and systematic theological statement made by Simone Weil is her attack, in the later pages of *The Need for Roots*, upon the dominance in Christian theology of the conception of a personal Providence. There she deploys a series of points, exegetical, historical, theological and philosophical, in support of her protest at the neglect of the conception of an impersonal Providence within the Christian church.

The points here include, but go far beyond, the rejection of the notion of God as sovereign which she believed to lie behind Ivan's rebellion. In the end she wished to circumscribe the notion of God as a person, insofar as it gave rise to a distorted and almost wholly mistaken account of providence:

> The conception of Providence which corresponds to God after the Roman style is that of a personal intervention in the world on the part of God in order to adjust certain means in view of certain particular ends.[40]

The conception gave rise to absurdities which she was not prepared to tolerate. For example it leads to the view that,

> God violates the natural order of the world so as to bring about therein, not what he wishes to produce, but causes which will produce what he wishes to produce by way of result.[41]

Why again, she asks, on this view, does someone who stands within feet of where lightning strikes, attribute his safety to a providential act of God whereas someone ten miles away does not? Even more crucially in the light of Ivan's discussion of suffering, if God is such that personal and providential interference in the natural order of things is possible, and does at times occur, why does it not occur on other occasions? On this view of God there are two possible sorts of reply: either God is completely capricious, or those who suffer do so at the specific command or at least permission of God. The former possibility is a picture of Nero rather than God, and the latter is what gave rise to the theology and imagery of Father Paneloux's first sermon in *The Plague*:

> See him there, that angel of pestilence, comely as Lucifer, shining like Evil's very self! He is hovering above your roofs with great spear in his right hand, poised to strike, while his left his hand is stretched towards one or other of your houses. Maybe at this very moment his finger is pointing to your door, the red spear crashing on its panels, and even now the plague is entering your home and settling down in your bedroom to await your return.[42]

Both these possibilities are incompatible with human sensitivity and with religious belief. True religious belief and the love of God are only possible if one is purged of such notions, and this is part of the background to the claims made in the *Notebooks* that there are two different forms of atheism, one of which is a *prolegomenon* to the love of God, 'a purification of the love of God'.

Even beyond the denial that God is rightly conceived of as a person, Simone Weil wished also to argue that there is a sense in which we must deny that God exists. There were a number of consequences which she believed to follow from belief in a person who exists called God, and all of these in their various ways serve only to obscure the true nature of God, and thus to deny the possibility of faith as she conceived it. Initially, as we have noticed, she believed that such a conception of God gave rise to absurdities at which the intellect rebelled. Secondly she believed that the conception of God as a person led to a serious misapplication of the notion of our being made in the image of God. She explains what she means in a condensed passage in *Waiting on God*.

There she argues that to speak of man as made in the image of God, is certainly to speak of *what has to do with* the fact that man is a person: but it is not *the fact itself* that a man is a person that is being spoken of here. What is being spoken of, is man's capacity to renounce his own personality, man's capacity to die to self and to live as one conformed to God, one in whom Christ lives. For Simone Weil the way of faith is the way of self-renunciation. Thus,

> It is then true in a sense that we must conceive of God as impersonal, in the sense that he is the divine model of a person who passes beyond the self by renunciation.[43]

perhaps then we should remodel our tree(?) of personhood?

At this point precisely lies her objection to the conception of an omnipotent and sovereign God. What that neglects is his self-emptying and self-renunciation. This latter she was attempting to clarify in terms of an understanding of God's relation to his creation, rather than solely in the more strictly christological emphasis to be found in a theologian such as P. T. Forsyth. There is no systematic statement on this in print, however, and I am inclined to think that this particular aspect of her thought had not developed much beyond embryonic stage.

Throughout the *Notebooks* are to be found a series of remarks which make it plain that there is a sense in which we must deny that God exists. Partly this is because the intelligence must have complete liberty, and insofar as it does it will not find itself led to affirm the existence of God. Such are the temptations open to the believer, that on occasions the only way of being sure that this liberty is not being wrongly and irreligiously infringed by the wrong sort of religious authoritarianism or through self-deception, is to allow the intelligence to affirm the conclusion that God does not exist. This, in itself, is not necessarily to draw nearer to God, but it can, and at times must, be part of the process of purification which is precondition of the love of God. The risk is that we may assume that through the use of the intelligence alone we may come to belief. The mistake there is to make the relationship between man and God one of affirmation and denial rather than of love. Simone Weil believed that contact with what is real does not come in the conclusion of an inductive or a deductive argument: it comes through the effective relation of love and desire. If this is true of the world, *a fortiori* it is true of God:

> The mysteries of faith cannot be either affirmed or denied; they must be placed above that which we affirm or deny.

> The intelligence must have complete liberty, including that of denying God; it follows from this that religion is related to love and not to affirmation or denial. For no good thing can harm the intelligence. But supernatural love, although its function is not to affirm, constitutes a fuller apprehension of reality than does the intelligence.[44]

Simone Weil believed that the reality in question was something *given*, and she argued in the light of the above that amongst those 'in whom the supernatural part of themselves' was not thus awakened, the atheists rather than those professing belief were right, were honest. If use of the intelligence could not lead one to belief, it was a step backwards rather than forwards to affirm the existence of God in wilful refusal of the findings of one's intelligence. One cannot compel belief in oneself or in any other.

A further consequence of affirming the existence of God against which Simone Weil rebelled can be brought out in the following way: she believed, to take a phrase used with considerable effect by Bonhoeffer, that we must live 'etsi deus non daretur'. There were three correlated dangers to which she believed we were exposed if we refused to live in this way. On the one hand we may stumble into the snare of acting only in the hope of

receiving some imagined reward or recompense, loving men for
the sake of God and the rewards which he might bestow, rather
than for the sake of themselves. The second danger is that we
begin to treat God and religion as a source of compensation and
consolation: 'religion', she argues, 'insofar as it is a source of consolation is a hindrance to true faith'. One of the greatest threats to
faith, she believed, was the risk of deceiving oneself into believing
that God existed, or that religious belief was not illusory because
one *needed* such a belief. Strong though such inclinations may be,
however, particularly, perhaps, amongst those who have been
born into a religious belief which they have not abandoned,
nonetheless it is fundamentally mistaken:

> . . . need is not a legitimate bond between Man and God.

> . . . For religious feeling to emanate from the spirit of truth,
> one should be absolutely prepared to abandon one's religion,
> even if that should mean losing all motive for living. In this
> state of mind alone is it possible to discern whether there is truth
> in it or not. Otherwise, one doesn't venture to propound the
> problem in all its rigour.[45]

There is in her approach to religious faith a rigour which reminds
one of Kant's account of the Holy Will, and which perhaps lets us
see what lay behind the nickname given with something less than
complete charity to Simone Weil by her fellow students – 'the
categorical imperative in skirts'.

The third danger of refusing to live 'etsi deus non daretur',
serves only to underline this demanding conception of faith. This
is the risk that from a belief in the existence of God we attempt to
derive beliefs which we use 'to fill up voids'. For example, into
this category comes the belief in immortality, the belief in the
usefulness of sins, the belief in the providential ordering of events.
What Simone Weil means by 'the void' is as difficult as it is
important for her thought, but it is only through the experience
of the void, of the limits of this world, and its lack of finality, that
a true conception of the possibility of faith can be had. In such
circumstances, the primary example of which for the Christian is

Christ's cry of dereliction, and only in such circumstances, does one perceive the limits beyond which one cannot pass: perhaps one may add, as Simone Weil did 'without supernatural aid', or perhaps one may not. Simone Weil's point is that one will not understand what such a remark may mean without experience of what she calls 'the void'.

Thus Simone Weil thought of certain sorts of atheism as a form of religious purification. But she is not advocating some sort of dialectical process whereby having in one sense denied the person and existence of God we go on in a different sense to affirm both of these. In this she differs quite markedly from many contemporary philosophers of religion for whom the nature of religious faith, and its opposite, is best understood in terms of the existence of a being as affirmed by the believer and denied by the atheist. Those who happily, but to some extent superficially substitute dictionary definition – ' "atheism" is the belief that God does not exist' – for philosophical reflection.

The mistakes which Simone Weil would see in that are twofold: on the one hand the view that the difference between atheist and believer is a difference in attitude to the proposition 'God exists', and on the other, the assumption that an account of religious belief can be given which ignores all effective attitudes.

One possible reason for this deficiency could be traced to what Simone Weil regarded as a lack of religious insight – the characterization of God as an all-powerful person. Of course, few philosophers would admit to such an elementary blunder, but even so, as Hume's *Dialogues* have shown us, it is incredibly difficult to avoid both anthropomorphism *and* the silence of agnosticism. If Simone Weil did succeed in avoiding both of these, and at the same time succeeded in escaping the charge of talking nonsense, then this was not achieved by following the path of so many of her theological contemporaries and offering an existential and anthropoligical account of the Christian faith. This too is of considerable significance for she moved quite counter to the prevailing theological winds in attempting to make what one can only call cosmological considerations central to her account of religious belief.

This comes out in part in the way in which, as we have noticed, she refused to accept the division asserted by Ivan between God and his creation. This division has in disguised form insinuated itself into a considerable number of contemporary theological writings. A consequence of this is that many religious thinkers have believed themselves to be in substantial agreement with those parts of Camus's thought which suggest that the environment in which men find themselves is indifferent in the sense of alien or even hostile. The notion of salvation which is then set alongside this is one whose central concept is self-awareness or self-knowledge, and often there is little attention given to the question of whether or not one's view of one's environment, of what used to be called 'creation', is meant to change in any way at all. Hence, as Simone Weil has argued, the supposed clash between religion and science comes on the religious side from the view that God and his creation can be separated.

But, of course, this is the hardest question, if they are not to be separated, what is one to make of the suffering of others?

> Necessity – an image which the intelligence can grasp representing God's indifference, his impartiality.[46]

A belief in an impersonal providence is a recognition that there are irreducible elements in this world – elements which, as irreducible, preclude the possibility of final ends and purposes being discerned or discovered in the world of space and time. Simone Weil did not want to deny that what we discover in our experience as being irreducible, unable to be transformed into something else, for example the bitterness of suffering undergone by oneself or another, must be recognized as such, and not viewed as a means to some finer end.

One way of putting the question is then, whether it is possible to take that view and also to see belief in God as anything other than in need of rejection. At that level her answer is affirmative. Strikingly, however, she wants to see suffering not as a potential barrier to belief, something *in spite of which* one still believes, but rather as something which is of the very essence of belief. In so far as this is the case the above quotation on 'necessity' does less than justice to parts of her thought. It might be taken as recommending some sort of intellectual consolation, a means of providing the intellectual reconciliation between the reality of suffering and the reality of God while still avoiding rebellion. That is considerably less than the truth of the matter: it *would* be the whole story if the God in question were a God conceived of now in this way – impersonal providence, now in that – personal providence, according to whether our fortunes fared well or ill, but Simone Weil will have no part of such intellectual sleight of hand.

Instead she makes central to her belief the notion of an impersonal providence. How, one might ask can the central religious notions of value and worship come into the picture? Here the difference between resignation to fate and *amor fati* has a role to play. But, again, one is forced to ask the sceptical question of whether such a conception can play any role at all in the spiritual life of the twentieth century? Perhaps such a question as this lies behind Roy Pierce's comment quoted earlier to the effect that it is Camus rather than Simone Weil who is more in harmony with his age.

What these two great spirits share, and what divides them most profoundly is inevitably best articulated in their own words; respectively, in this instance from early pages of *The Rebel*, and the closing pages of *The Need for Roots*:

> The rebel is a man who is on the point of accepting or rejecting the sacred and determined on laying claim to a human situation in which all the answers are human – in other words, formulated on reasonable terms. From this moment, every question, every word is an act of grace. It would be possible to demonstrate in this manner that only two possible worlds exist for the human mind: the sacred (or, to speak in Christian terms, the world of grace) and the world of rebellion. The disappearance of one is equivalent to the appearance of the other . . . Is it possible to find a rule of conduct outside the realm of religion and its absolute values? That is the question roused by rebellion![47]

> Brute force is not sovereign in this world. It is by nature blind and indeterminate. What is sovereign in this world is deter-

minateness limit. Eternal wisdom imprisons this universe in a network, a web of determinations. The universe accepts passively. The brute force of matter, which appears to us sovereign, is nothing else in reality but perfect obedience.[48]

The order of the world is the same as the beauty of the world. All that differs is the type of concentration demanded, according to whether one tries to conceive the necessary relations which go to make it up or to contemplate its splendour.[49]

The order of the world is to be loved because it is pure obedience to God. Whatever this universe accords or inflicts on us, it does so exclusively out of obedience.[50]

Which of these two is then the more in harmony with our age – Camus who speaks in the accent of protest and rebellion, or Simone Weil who tells us that ultimately fulfilment is to be found in love of the order of the world?

They shared a sense of the importance of the sacred, but in the end Camus preaches rebellion. They agree that 'brute force is not sovereign', but their sense of what lies at the limits – 'les limites' – diverges radically.

Perhaps the first lesson which they teach us is that the heart of European culture centres round the religious and philosophical questions whose history stretches over more than two and a half thousand years. Whether one accepts or rejects the idea of the sacred, of grace, spirits as rare as those of Simone Weil and Albert Camus belong to a common inheritance which theologians or humanists dismiss at their peril. The philistines who think that we have left such questions behind whether speaking the language of a false scientism or of a self-confident social engineer are squandering their spiritual heritage. Equally mistaken are those theologians who have reduced their craft to a series of specialisms which neatly exclude from the picture the central continuing concerns of European culture – the nature of human fulfilment, the presence of evil and suffering, the aweful beauty of the world in which we live.

POSTSCRIPT

The four studies presented in this volume are individually and communally offered as examples which will help us to begin to define the many ambiguities and forms of ambiguity which arise from working in the borderlands between belief and unbelief. In the nature of the case what is offered is a variety, but some points of a more general nature may be made in postscript, to underline certain continuities.

Dostoyevsky and Hume raise two fundamental questions about faith. In his novels are reflected Dostoyevsky's continuing preoccupation with the question of whether the life of faith or sainthood can be given recognizable, particular form. To this was added Hume's question of whether the dispute between belief and unbelief is in the end 'mere verbal controversy'.

Kierkegaard implicitly answers both of these questions and does so by asking us whether faith lies in indirectness, and hiddenness. If the answer to that is positive, then we may allow that as Hume suggests argument over the content of belief is 'mere verbal controversy', *but* only if we restrict communication to direct communication – only if we mistakenly believe that we may describe or depict the transcendent. If however, we do not fall into this error, we will see that Dostoyevsky's literary hope of the portrayal of sainthood is bound to come to naught.

This of course, does not resolve all of our problems, for as the discussion proceeds we see that what it serves to do is to define the question which ties together both Simone Weil and Albert Camus – the question of whether there is 'un style die vie' appropriate to the twentieth century, and whether if there be such it includes or excludes religious belief. From different bivouacs in the borderlands Simone Weil and Albert Camus offer us alternative answers. Camus hopes to make central the concept of rebellion, Simone Weil that of obedience: ultimately Simone Weil believes we must in some sense accept suffering, whereas Camus affirms himself over against suffering. The differences are profound, but for all that linked by the gossamer threads of mutual respect and a common acknowledgment of the realities of a suffering world.

Such respect 'across the border' is to be found explicitly and implicitly in all of our examples. This is because of a common intellectual and spiritual heritage, and a shared insistence that any 'style of life' must be provisional and exploratory in character. The religious expression for this is pilgrimage, and spiritual pilgrimage and intellectual pilgrimage go hand in hand.

The awareness of the importance of the category of pilgrimage lies in the stress to be found in each of our case studies, on human finitude. In the case of Dostoyevsky this led to a stress upon process and possibly progress, rather than *telos*. Hume's stress upon (albeit 'mitigated') scepticism hardly needs underlining and Kierkegaard's respect for scepticism, although not unbounded was a natural *prolegomenon* to a preoccupation with the tension between an infinite or transcendent focus of faith, and a finite believing soul. The consequence was the ambiguity and hiddenness of indirectness being offered as the appropriate form of faith.

Finally the options for 'un style de vie' offered to us respectively by Simone Weil and Albert Camus each also stress human finitude. Camus uses this as a stick to beat overt and self-confident religion, but he rejects also aspiration to superhumanity, and insists that there are 'mysteries' still to enumerate. Simone Weil's own halting spiritual and intellectual pilgrimage is itself a parable of the recognition of finitude in search of the infinite.

Perhaps the phenomena which we have been examining will appear excessively intellectual to those muscular souls for whom issues of belief or unbelief are clear and unambiguous. To these there is little else to say other than that thinking always includes the possibility of thinking again.

NOTES

1. Dostoyevsky

1. References are to *The Brothers Karamazov*, trans. Constance Garnett, Heinemann 1968.

2. P. Rahv, 'The Sources and Significance of "The Legend of the Grand Inquisitor"', in E. Wasiolek (ed.), *The Brothers Karamazov and the Critics*, Wadsworth 1967.

3. G. Steiner, *Tolstoy or Dostoyevsky*, Penguin Books 1967.

4. R. Guardini, 'The Legend of the Grand Inquisitor', *Cross Currents*, vol. iii, 1952.

5. See V. Rozanov, *Dostoevsky and the Legend of the Grand Inquisitor*, Cornell University Press 1972.

6. K. Mochulsky, *Dostoyevsky, His Life and Work*, trans. Michael E. Minihan, Princeton University Press 1967, p. xix.

7. Letter of 15 October 1880, to P. Ye. Guseva, quoted in Mochulsky, op. cit., p. 644.

8. See Jessie Coulson, *Dostoyevsky: A Self-Portrait*, Oxford University Press 1962, letter 144, p. 228.

9. Dostoyevsky, *The Devils*, trans. D. Magarshack, Penguin Books 1953, pp. 505–6.

10. *The Diary of a Writer*, trans. Boris Brasol, George Braziller, New York 1954.

11. Karl Barth, *The Epistle to the Romans*, trans. Edwyn Hoskyns, Oxford University Press 1933.

12. Eduard Thurneysen, *Dostoyevsky*, trans. K. R. Crim, Epworth Press 1964.

13. *Diary of a Writer*, p. 984.

14. See *Letters of Fyodor Dostoyevsky*, trans. E. C. Mayne, McGraw-Hill 1964, p. 219.

15. *Diary of a Writer*, p. 286, my italics.

16. *Letters*, p. 277.

17. Thurneysen, op. cit., pp. 43–4.

18. *Diary of a Writer*, p. 365.

19. *Essays and Aphorisms*, trans. R. J. Hollingdale, Penguin Books 1970, pp. 223–4.

20. Coulson, op. cit., pp. 224–5.

21. Thurneysen, op. cit., pp. 12–13.

22. *Crime and Punishment*, trans. David Magarshack, Penguin Books 1951.

23. *Letters*, p. 142.

24. *Letters from the Underworld*, trans. C. J. Hogarth, Everyman Library, Dent 1964.

2. David Hume

1. See E. C. Mossner, *The Life of David Hume*, Oxford University Press 1970, p. 483.

2. Alexander Carlyle, *Anecdotes and Characters of the Times*, ed. J. Kinsley, Oxford University Press 1973.

3. See *The Letters of David Hume*, ed. J. Y. T. Greig, Oxford University Press 1932, vol. I, p. 154.

4. Quotations are from David Hume, *Dialogues Concerning Natural Religion*, ed. N. Kemp Smith, Oxford 1947, reissued Bobbs-Merrill 1970.

5. See N. Pike (ed.), *Dialogues Concerning Natural Religion*, Bobbs-Merrill 1970; N. Capaldi, 'Hume's Philosophy of Religion', *International Journal of the Philosophy of Religion*, 1970; N. Kemp Smith, op. cit.; J. C. Gaskin, *Hume's Philosophy of Religion*, Macmillan 1978; T. Penelhum, *Hume*, Macmillan 1978.

6. See J. Wisdom, 'Gods', *Proceedings of the Aristotelian Society*, 1944–5.

7. I have elucidated and discussed these issues more fully in 'Hume on Morality and the Emotions', *Philosophical Quarterly*, vol. 26, 1976.

3. Sören Kierkegaard

1. E. Brunner, *The Philosophy of Religion*, Ivor Nicholson and Watson, London 1931.

2. S. Kierkegaard, *Philosophical Fragments*, Princeton University Press 1962; *Concluding Unscientific Postscript*, Princeton University Press 1941.

3. *Concluding Unscientific Postscript*, p. 67.

4. Ibid., p. 66.

5. Cf. Kierkegaard, *The Present Age*, Harper & Row 1962, p. 25.

6. *Concluding Unscientific Postscript*, p. 271.

7. *The Point of View of My Work as Author*, trans. W. Lowrie, Oxford University Press 1950, p. 76.

8. Ibid., p. 8.

9. Cf. G. E. and G. B. Arbaugh, *Kierkegaard's Authorship*, Allen & Unwin 1968, p. 95.

10. *The Point of View*, p. 71.

11. Kierkegaard, *Either/Or*, trans. Swenson and Lowrie, Doubleday 1959; *Fear and Trembling*, trans. Lowrie, Princeton University Press 1945.

12. See *The Point of View*, p. 22.

13. Ibid.

14. 'Appropriation' is a technical term in Kierkegaard used to express the nature of one's relationship to truth. Its positive content will become clearer as we proceed, but initially its negative content is a rejection of the view that what is true of men is wholly expressible in propositions to which we may give varying degrees of assent.

15. See 'A First and Last Declaration', printed following p. 550 in the English translation of *Concluding Unscientific Postscript*.

16. *The Point of View*, p. 72.

17. *The Present Age*, p. 64.

18. That Kierkegaard talks at all of the value or health of community is often forgotten in the wake of his emphasis upon the individual. That emphasis should be seen as a response to what he regarded as the follies of his age, not as an absolute rejection of the possibility of an ethical or religious *community*.

19. *Fear and Trembling*, p. 5.

20. Ibid., p. 42.

21. *The Point of View*, p. 24.

22. Ibid., p. 40.

23. *The Present Age*, p. 3.

24. Ibid., p. 72.

25. *Concluding Unscientific Postscript*, p. 368.

26. Ibid., p. 110.

27. Ibid., p. 119.

28. Ibid., p. 268.

29. Ibid., p. 281.

30. Ibid., p. 120.

31. Ibid., pp. 121–2.

32. Cf. ibid., p. 221. 'Precisely as important as the truth, and if one of the two is to be emphasized, still more important, is the manner in which the truth is accepted.'

33. Kierkegaard argues in *Philosophical Fragments* that arguments of this sort always tacitly assume the existence of God as one of the premisses.

34. *Concluding Unscientific Postscript*, p. 178.

35. Ibid., p. 221.

36. Ibid., p. 582.

37. Ibid., p. 178.

38. Ibid., p. 72.

39. Ibid., p. 75.

40. Ibid.

41. Ibid., p. 311.

42. Ibid., p. 28.

43. Ibid., p. 268.

44. In a strict sense Kant did not deal with this dilemma as he dealt with the

Antinomies in the *Critique of Pure Reason*. See his discussion in the *Critique of Practical Reason*, trans. L. W. Beck, Bobbs-Merrill 1956, pp. 128–36.

45. R. W. Hepburn, *Christianity and Paradox*, Watts 1958, p. 17.

46. R. F. Holland, 'Morality and the Two Worlds Concept' in I. T. Ramsey (ed.), *Christian Ethics and Contemporary Philosophy*, SCM Press 1966, pp. 302f.

47. *Concluding Unscientific Postscript*, pp. 320–1.

48. Ibid., p. 137.

49. *Purity of Heart is to Will One Thing*, trans. Douglas V. Steere, Harper & Row 1956.

50. *Purity of Heart*, p. 54.

51. Ibid., p. 202.

52. Ibid., pp. 25 and 36.

53. Ibid., pp. 184 and 186.

54. *The Last Years*, ed., R. Gregor Smith, Fontana Books 1968, p. 317.

55. Ibid., pp. 300–1.

4. Simone Weil and Albert Camus

1. C. Milosz, 'The Importance of Simone Weil' (1960) reprinted in his *The Emperor of the Earth*, University of California Press 1981. (I am indebted to Andrew Noble for drawing this reference to my attention.)

2. See Albert Camus, *The Outsider*, English translation, Stuart Gilbert, Hamish Hamilton 1957; Penguin Books 1961, pp. 117–18.

3. Albert Camus, *The Rebel*, English translation, Anthony Power, Hamish Hamilton 1953; Penguin Books 1962, p. 27.

4. S. Weil, *Gravity and Grace*, Routledge & Kegan Paul 1963, pp. 35–8.

5. S. Weil, *First and Last Notebooks*, Oxford University Press 1970, p. 83.

6. *The Rebel*, p. 51.

7. *First and Last Notebooks*, p. 82.

8. Albert Camus, *The Plague*, trans. Stuart Gilbert, Hamish Hamilton 1948; Penguin Books 1960, p. 83.

9. S. Weil, *The Need for Roots*, Routledge & Kegan Paul 1952.

10. The review is reprinted in Albert Camus, *Essais*, Bibliotheque de la Pleiade, Gallimard 1965, p. 1700.

11. See Roy Pierce, *Contemporary French Political Thought*, Oxford University Press 1966, p. 121.

12. Jean Grenier, *Albert Camus (Souvenirs)*, Gallimard 1964, p. 31.

13. See Camus, *Carnets, 1942–51*, Gallimard 1964, p. 31.

14. Ibid., p. 162.

15. Ibid., p. 21.

16. *The Rebel*, p. 51.

17. *Carnets, 1942–51*, p. 31.

18. *The Need for Roots*, p. 239.

19. See S. Weil, 'The Power of Words', *Selected Essays, 1934–43*, Oxford University Press 1962.

20. S. Weil, *On Science, Necessity and the Loved God*, Oxford University Press 1968, p. 65.

21. *Carnets, 1942–51*, p. 247.

22. *The Plague*, p. 136.

23. S. Weil, *Waiting on God*, Routledge & Kegan Paul 1951; Fontana 1959, p. 63.

24. S. Weil, *Notebooks*, 2 vols, Routledge & Kegan Paul 1976, p. 31.

25. *The Plague*, pp. 106–8.

26. *The Need for Roots*, p. 6.

27. Ibid., p. 275.

28. *Carnets II*, p. 341.

29. *Notebooks*, vol. 1, p. 288.

30. *Waiting on God*, p. 55.

31. *Notebooks*, vol. 1, p. 283.

32. Ibid., p. 291.

33. *The Rebel*, p. 16, my italics.

34. *Notebooks*, vol. 1, p. 287.

35. *The Plague*, p. 107.

36. *Waiting on God*, pp. 160–1.

37. *Notebooks*, vol. 1, p. 297.

38. Ibid., p. 299.

39. Ibid., p. 305.

40. *The Need for Roots*, p. 267.

41. Ibid.

42. *The Plague*, p. 81.

43. *Waiting on God*, p. 133.

44. *Notebooks*, vol. 1, pp. 234 and 242.

45. *The Need for Roots*, pp. 237 and 239.

46. *Notebooks*, vol. 1, p. 297.

47. See *The Rebel*, pp. 26–7.

48. *The Need for Roots*, p. 272.

49. Ibid., p. 281.

50. Ibid., p. 275.

INDEX OF NAMES